250

D0840359

EASY JAPANESE

by the same author

ESSENTIAL JAPANESE
KOREAN IN A HURRY
BASIC JAPANESE CONVERSATION DICTIONARY

EASY JAPANESE

A
Direct Approach
To Immediate Conversation

Third Revised Edition

by

SAMUEL E. MARTIN

Professor of Far Eastern Linguistics
Yale University

CHARLES E. TUTTLE CO.
Rutland, Vermont
Tokyo, Japan

1/95

KAWASAKI READING ROOM UNL

Representatives

For Continental Europe:
BOXERBOOKS, INC., *Zurich*

For the British Isles:
PRENTICE-HALL INTERNATIONAL, INC., *London*

For Australasia:
PAUL FLESCH & CO., PTY. LTD., *Melbourne*

For Canada:
HURTIG PUBLISHERS, *Edmonton*

*Published by the Charles E. Tuttle Company, Inc.
of Rutland, Vermont & Tokyo, Japan
with editorial offices at Suido 1-chome, 2-6
Bunkyo-ku, Tokyo, Japan*

*Copyright in Japan, 1957, by
Charles E. Tuttle Co., Inc.*

All rights reserved

Library of Congress Catalog Card No. 57-6763

International Standard Book No. 0-8048-0157-6

*First printing, 1957
Fifth printing, 1959
Second edition (revised and enlarged), 1959
Sixth printing, 1962
Third edition (revised), 1962
Twenty-seventh printing, 1974*

Printed in Japan

CONTENTS

Introduction vii

Part 1: Say It with a Word—or Two

Lesson 1. Hello and Goodbye 3
Lesson 2. Excuse Me, Thank you,
          and Please 5
Lesson 3. Who? 9
Lesson 4. What? 13
Lesson 5. Have You Got Any? 16
Lesson 6. Where? 20
Lesson 7. Whose? 24
Lesson 8. When? 28
Lesson 9. How Much? 33
Lesson 10. How Many? How Old? .. 37
Lesson 11. How Many People?...... 41
Lesson 12. What Time? 45
Lesson 13. How Long?............. 49

Part II: Add a Bit of Action

Lesson 14. Did You? 57
Lesson 15. Do You? Will you?...... 61
Lesson 16. Shall We? Let's 66
Lesson 17. What Kind? 69
Lesson 18. Is, Am, and Are 73

CONTENTS

Lesson 19. What's Doing? 77
Lesson 20. Please Do! 83

Part III: Sprinkle in a Few Particles

Lesson 21. Where From? Where To?.. 91
Lesson 22. Where Shall We Eat? 96
Lesson 23. Me Too; Me Neither 101
Lesson 24. Who Does What? 103
Lesson 25. A Sentence Opener (*wa*)..107
Lesson 26. What Did You Say? 112
Lesson 27. Is It or Isn't It? 117
Lesson 28. Can You? Probably 121
Lesson 29. Because and But 124
Lesson 30. How To Be Emphatic 128

Part IV: 3000 Useful Japanese Words 133

Part V: Writing Charts 267

vi

INTRODUCTION

This little book will have you talking Japanese in no time at all. Each lesson presents a few of the most common features of the language in sentences which are short, easy, and immediately useful. The first thirteen lessons show you there is a lot that can be said with just a word or two. The later lessons introduce more variety and explain a few of the fine points. I have tried to keep the sentences short but colloquial, abrupt but not rude. Each lesson contains first a number of PHRASES; these should be memorized. There is only one way to learn a language, and that is to TALK it. As soon as you have memorized a phrase, START USING IT. Once you know how to say "hello" and "goodbye" in Japanese, never let a Japanese hear you use English in those situations. Japanese are pleased to hear you talk their language, and the more you talk it, the better you will get along. After the phrases, there is some material for PRACTICE. These are short conversations made up entirely of the phrases you have learned in the lesson (or in preceding lessons). Each of these conversations is built around a rather simple situation; see if you can figure the situation out. Finally there are some TIPS to help you learn the material and to tell you a few other things helpful in talking with your Japanese friends. A key to the practice exercise is included at the end of each lesson. You should consult this only after you have tried to puzzle out the exercise without it. After looking at the key, go back and practice the exercise again. Try to get the situation in Japanese terms, not English ones.

After the lessons, there is a basic vocabulary of some common Japanese words and their English equivalents. In this, the Japanese verbs are presented both in the polite present (**-mas'**) and the plain present (**-u** or **-ru**). When the two forms would come close together in alphabetical order, they are given on one line; in other cases, you will see two entries. You will find it useful to get a copy of the author's forthcoming BASIC JAPANESE CONVERSATION DICTIONARY. This dictionary, in addition to a Japanese-English part, includes 3000 common English words with their Japanese equivalents in both Romanization and Japanese writing.

At the end of the book there are some charts of Japanese writing. When you have finished the lessons, you may want to learn to read some of the simple symbols you see on the signs around you.

The Japanese is presented in a modified

version of the Hepburn romanization. Most
of the consonants are pronounced about as
in English, the vowels as in Italian: **a** as in
f*a*ther, e as in m*e*t or y*e*s, i as in mar*i*ne
or macaron*i*, o as in s*o*lo or P*o*go, u as in
r*u*le or L*u*l*u*. These vowels are shorter than
our English vowels; the long varieties
(marked **ā, ō, ū, ii,** and **ei** or **ē**) are a
little longer and tenser than the English
sounds like them. In everyday speech, many
final long vowels are shortened. The apos-
trophe (as in **s'koshi arimas'**) represents a
short **u** or **i** which is suppressed in ordinary
speech. The tongue is pushed farther forward (against the teeth) for Japanese **t, d,**
and **n** than for the English sounds. The
Japanese **r** may sound like a combination
of **r, l,** and **d** to you. Your English **d**
(if you say it very quick) is probably the
closest. But don't mix it up with a Japanese
d! The Japanese **g** never has the "soft"
j- sound as in *g*em or *g*in; it is either
"hard" as in *g*et or *g*ift or it has the "ng"
sound in sin*g*er. If you have trouble with
the "ng" version, forget it and use the
"hard" g everywhere. The **n** which comes
at the end of a word sounds a little bit like
a weak "ng" instead of a full-fledged **n**;
try to imitate this if you hear the difference.

If you want to find out more about Japanese, get a copy of the author's complete
textbook ESSENTIAL JAPANESE. This explains

the grammar in more detail and gives many additional examples. You might like to continue your study of Japanese with that book when you have finished this.

PART I

Say It with a Word—or Two

Lesson 1

HELLO AND GOODBYE

Phrases

Good morning.	**Ohayō.**
Hello (during the day).	**Konnichi wa.**
Hello (in the evening).	**Komban wa.**
Goodbye.	**Sayonara.**
Good night.	**Oyasumi nasai.**
So long. (*or* See you later.)	**Mata.** (or **Mata ne.** or **Mata aimashō.**)
Hello (on the telephone).	**Moshi moshi.**
Hey!	**Moshi moshi.**
Uh... (*or* Hey! *or* Say!)	**Ano ne.**
Hey! (*or* Just a minute please!)	**Chotto.**
Yes.	**Hai.** (or **Ē.**)
No.	**Iie.**

3

PRACTICE

A: Ohayō. B: Ohayō.... A: Mata ai-mashō. B: Hai. Sayonara.

A: Konnichi wa. B: Konnichi wa.... A: Ano ne. B: Hai.... A: Sayonara. B: Sayonara. Mata aimashō.

A: Moshi moshi. B: Moshi moshi. A: Ano ne. B: Hai. A: *Mister Smith?* B: Iie. *Brown.* A: Sayonara. B: Sayonara.

A: Moshi moshi! Ano ne! Chotto! Chotto! B: Hai.

A: Komban wa. B: Komban wa.... A: Sayonara. Oyasumi nasai. B: Oyasumi nasai. Sayonara.

A: Mata aimashō. Oyasumi nasai. B: Hai. Oyasumi nasai.

TIPS

Try not to stare at a Japanese when you talk to him. Many Japanese feel it is rude to look a person directly in the face; "if the person has an ugly face, he will feel uncomfortable"—this is the way it was once explained. The Japanese are very considerate not to hurt other people's feelings.

A: Good morning. *B*: Good morning.... *A*: See you later. B: OK—goodbye.

A: Hello. *B*: Hello... *A*: Say.... *B*: Yes.... A: Goodbye. B: Goodbye—see you later.

A: Hello. *B*: Hello. *A*: Uh.... *B*: Yes. *A*: Mister Smith? *B*: No. Brown. *A*: Goodbye. *B*: Goodbye.

A: Hey! Say there! Just a minute! Hey there! *B*: Yes.

A: Good evening. *B*: Good evening.... *A*: Goodbye. Goodnight. *B*: Goodnight. Goodbye.

A: See you later. Goodnight. *B*: Yes. Goodnight.

Lesson 2

EXCUSE ME, THANK YOU, AND PLEASE

PHRASES

Excuse me. (*or* Thank you.)	Sumimasen. (or Dōmo sumimasen. or Dōmo.)
Not at all.	Iie. (or Dō itashimash'te.)
Excuse me.	Gomen nasai. (or Gomen nasai ne.)
I've been rude.	Shitsure(i). (or Shitsurei shimash'ta.)
A little bit.	Chotto.
Excuse me a moment.	Chotto shitsurei.

5

Please wait a min-ute.	Chotto matte. (or Chotto matte kudasai.)
Please.	Dōzo.
Please come again.	Mata dōzo.
Thank you.	Arigato. (or Arigato gozaimas'. or Dōmo arigato.)
Hello — anybody home?	Gomen kudasai! (said at front door)

PRACTICE

A: Sumimasen. B: Iie.

A: Sumimasen. Dōmo. B: Iie. Dō itashimash'te.

A: Arigato. Dōmo arigato. B: Iie, iie.

A: Chotto shitsurei. B: Hai, dōzo.
A: Sumimasen. B: Iie.

A: Gomen kudasai! B: Hai. Konnichi wa. A: Konnichi wa. *Mister Brown?* B: Hai, dōzo. A: Shitsurei, shitsurei. B: Dōzo, dōzo. . . . A: Dōmo sumimasen. B: Iie, shitsurei. Gomen nasai. A: Dōmo. Sayonara. B: Sayonara. Mata dōzo.

A: Moshi moshi. B: Moshi moshi. A: Ano ne. B: Hai. A: Nikkatsu Hotel? B: Iie. A: Sumimasen. Dōmo. Gomen nasai. B: Iie. Dō itashimashite. Sayo-

6

nara. A: Sayonara.

A: **Moshi moshi.** B: **Moshi moshi.**
A: **Ano ne.** B: **Hai.** A: **Nikkatsu Hotel?**
B: **Hai.** A: **Sumimasen.** *Mister Clark?*
B: **Hai, hai. Chotto matte. Chotto shitsurei. Dōzo.** C: **Moshi moshi.** A: **Moshi
moshi.** *Mister Clark?* C: **Hai.** A: **Gomen nasai. Ano ne....** A: **Arigato gozaimas'.** C: **Dō itashimash'te. Shitsurei
shimash'ta.** A: **Iie. Dōmo sumimasen.
Sayonara.** C: **Sayonara. Oyasumi nasai.**

TIPS

The Japanese spend much of their time
excusing themselves and thanking you. Perhaps this may strike you as a little silly at
first, but if you play the game you will find
it makes everybody feel very good. When
Americans say "thank you" or "excuse
me" it is one time at most—Japanese say
them at least ONCE in every conversation,
and usually TWO or THREE times. There
are a great many different ways to say these
things in Japanese; some are restricted to
special situations. Whenever you feel something should be said, but don't know quite
what to say, try either **Sumimasen** or **Dōmo**
—they cover everything. And be prepared
to come back with **Iie** or **Dō itashimash'te**
(or both) whenever someone says something
nice to you. You will notice the Japanese

7

do a lot of bowing from the waist. They don't expect you to be quite so formal, but a humble bob of the head every now and then will show that your "excuse me" or "thank you" is more than an empty phrase.

A: Excuse me. (*or* Thank you.) *B*: Not at all.

A: Excuse me. Terribly sorry. (*or* Thank you. Ever so much.) *B*: Not at all. Think nothing of it.

A: Thank you. Thanks a lot. *B*: That's all right, think nothing of it.

A: Excuse me a minute. *B*: Surely, go right ahead. *A*: I'm sorry. *B*: Not at all.

A: Excuse me—anybody home? *B*: Yes ("Coming—"). Good afternoon. *A*: Good afternoon. (Are you) Mr. Brown? *B*: Yes. Please (come in). *A*: Excuse me (for intruding). *B*: Please, please (come right in).... *A*: Thank you ever so much. *B*: Not at all, I've been rude. Excuse me. *A*: Thanks. Goodbye. *B*: Goodbye. Please come again.

A: Hello. *B*: Hello. *A*: Uh.... *B*: Yes? *A*: (Is this the) Nikkatsu Hotel? *B*: No. *A*: Sorry. Ever so sorry. Excuse me. *B*: Not at all. Think nothing of it. Goodbye. *A*: Goodbye.

A: Hello. *B*: Hello. *A*: Uh.... *B*: Yes? *A*: (Is this the) Nikkatsu Hotel? *B*: Yes. *A*: Excuse me. (Is) Mister Clark (there)? *B*: Yes sir. Wait just a minute. Excuse me a minute. Please (go ahead now). *C*: Hello. *A*: Hello. (Are you) Mister Clark? *C*: Yes. *A*: Excuse me. Uh.... *A*: Thank you. *C*: Not at all. I've been rude. *A*: Not at all. Thank you (*or* excuse me) ever so much. Goodbye. *C*: Goodbye. Goodnight.

8

Lesson 3

WHO?

PHRASES

who?	**dare?** (or **donata?**)
you	**anata** (or **anta**)
me, I	**watak'shi** (or **watashi**)
him, he	**ano hito** (or **kare**)
her, she	**ano hito** (or **kano-jo**)
them, they	**ano hito** (or **ano hito-tachi**)
us, we	**watashi-tachi**
you all	**mina-san**
wife (or lady of the house or madam)	**ok'-san**
my wife	**kanai**
husband (or master or boss)	**danna-san** (or **shujin**)
Mr. Tanaka Mrs. Tanaka Miss Tanaka	**Tanaka san**
Dr. Tanaka	**Tanaka sense(i)**
the doctor	**isha** (or **o-isha-san**)
the maid	**jochū** (or **jochū san**)
the teacher	**sense(i)**
the schoolboy	**gak'se(i)** (or **gak'sei san**)

9

the soldier	**heitai** (or **heitai san**)
the friend	**tomodachi**
the American	**Amerika-jin**
the Japanese	**Nihon-jin**
the Englishman	**Eikoku-jin**
the merchant (*or* trader)	**shōnin**
Is that so? (*or* Oh? How interest-ing! *or* I see!)	**Sō des' ka?**
How do you do!	**Hajimemash'te.**
How do you do! (*or* Please get ac-quainted!)	**Dōzo yorosh'ku.**

PRACTICE

A: **Anata—dare?** B: **Watashi—Tana-ka.** A: **Anata—Amerika-jin?** B: **Iie, Nihon-jin.** A: **Sō des' ka?** **Ok'-san?** B: **Kano-jo — Nihon-jin.** **Anata?** A: **Watashi—Amerika-jin. Watashi—Tōkyō; kanai—Amerika**

A: **Chotto sumimasen. Anata—Eikoku-jin?** B: **Iie. Watashi—Amerika-jin.** A: **Sō des' ka? Sumimasen. Watashi— Nihon-jin, Tanaka, isha. Anata—dare?** B: **Sō des' ka? Hajimemash'te. Watashi —*Brown*, heitai.** A: **Hajimemash'te. Dō-zo yorosh'ku.** B: **Dōzo yorosh'ku.** A:

10

Shitsurei, ok'-san—? B: Kanai—Amerika. A: Sumimasen. Mata aimashō. B: Hai. Dōmo. Gomen nasai. Sayonara. A: Sayonara. Gomen nasai.

A: Gomen kudasai. Maid: Hai, hai. A: Sumimasen. Tanaka sensei? Maid: Hai. Chotto shitsurei.... Mrs. Tanaka: Sumimasen. Dōmo shitsurei. A: Iie, iie. Kano-jo dare? Mrs. T: Kano-jo? Kano-jo—jochū.... Dōzo. A: Shitsurei. Dōmo. Danna-san? T: Danna-san—Ginza, shopping-u. Gomen nasai. A: Sō des' ka? Dō itashimashite.

A: Ano hito—dare? B: Gak'sei. A: Sō des' ka? Watashi—gak'sei. B: Sō desu ka? Kare—tomodachi. Dōzo. A: Dōmo arigato. Sumimasen. B: Dō itashimash'te.... Tanaka san, *Andrews* san. Dozo yorosh'ku. T: Hajimemash'te. Dōzo yorosh'ku. A: Dōzo yorosh'ku. Hajimemash'te. T: *Andrews* san—sensei? A: Iie, gak'sei. T: Amerika-jin? A: Hai. Amerika-jin, gak'sei. T: *Brown* san—gak'sei san? A: Iie, kare—heitai san.

TIPS

When you cannot make yourself understood—DON'T SHOUT. This is not only very rude, it makes you harder to understand.

Slow down, go back, and try to say the same thing with different words. Most Japanese know quite a lot of individual English words but they are not used to hearing them pronounced and used in sentences. When you don't understand a Japanese, excuse yourself and say **Mō ichido** "again" or **Yukkuri** "slowly." When you don't know a Japanese word, use an English word, but say it slowly and try to imitate the way a Japanese would pronounce it. As regards **anata** or **anta** "you" and **watak'shi** or **watashi** "me," the longer forms are the more standard, while the shorter forms are on the informal side.

A: You—who (are you)? *B*: Me—(I'm) Tanaka. *A*: You—(are you) an American? *B*: No, a Japanese. *A*: Well well. Your wife? *B*: Her—(she's) a Japanese. (How about) you? *A*: Me—(I'm) an American. Me—(I'm in) Tokyo; my wife—(she's) in America.

A: Excuse me a minute. You—(are you) English? *B*: No. Me—(I'm) an American. *A*: Oh? Excuse me. Me—(I'm) a Japanese, Tanaka (by name), a doctor (by profession). You—who (are you)? *B*: Well well. How do you do. Me—(I'm) Brown, a soldier. *A*: How do you do. My compliments. *B*: My compliments. *A*: Excuse me (for asking a rude question but) your wife—? *B*: My wife—(as for her it's) America. (My wife is in America. *or* My wife is an American.) *A*: Thank you. So long. *B*: Yes. Thank you. Excuse me. Goodbye. *A*: Goodbye. Excuse me.

A: Excuse me—anybody home? *Maid*: Yes, yes ("coming—"). *A*: Excuse me. Dr. Tanaka (is he

12

home)? *Maid*: Yes (I understand what you want), just a minute please.... *Mrs. Tanaka*: Excuse me. I've been very rude. *A*: Not at all. Her—who (is she)? *Mrs. T.*: Her? Her—(she's) the maid.... Please (come in). *A*: Excuse me. Sorry. Your husband (is he here)? *T.*: My husband—(he's in) Ginza, shopping. I'm sorry. *A*: Oh? That's all right—think nothing of it.

A: Him—who (is he)? *B*: A student. *A*: Really? Me—(I'm) a student. *B*: Oh? Him—(he is) a friend (of mine). Please (let me introduce you). *A*: Thanks very much. Thank you. B: Not at all. ...Mr. Tanaka, Mr. Andrews. Please get acquainted. *T*: How do you do. My compliments. *A*: My compliments. How do you do. *T*: Mr. Andrews—(are you) a teacher? *A*: No, a student. *T*: An American? *A*: Yes, (I'm) an American student. *T*: Mr. Brown—(is he) a student? *A*: No, him—(he's) a soldier.

Lesson 4

WHAT?

PHRASES

what?	nani?
cigarettes	tabako
matches	matchi
food	tabemono
bread	pan
meat	niku
vegetables	yasai

water	**mizu**
beer	**biiru**
sake (rice wine)	**o-sake**
milk	**miruku**
coffee	**kōhii**
Japanese tea	**o-cha**
black tea	**kōcha**
pencil	**empitsu**
book	**hon**
table	**tēburu**
chair	**isu**
clothes	**kimono**
American clothes	**yōf'ku**
Japanese clothes	**waf'ku**
ticket	**kippu**
this one	**kore**
this...	**kono...**
that one (near you)	**sore**
that...	**sono...**
that one over there	**are**
that...	**ano...**
which one?	**dore?**
which...?	**dono...?**

PRACTICE

A: **Kore—nani?** B: **Sore—tabako. Dō-zo.** A: **Arigato. Matchi?** B: **Hai, dōzo.** A: **Sumimasen.** B: **Iie.** A: **Mizu? Biiru? Miruku?** B: **Miruku.** A: **Hai. dōzo.**

B: **Dōmo**.

A: **Ano ne.** B: **Hai.** A: **Kore—nani?**
B: **Sore—kimono.** A: **Sō desu ka? Yō-
f'ku?** B: **Iie, waf'ku.**

A: **Kono hon—nani?** B: **Sono hon—**
textbook (**tekis'to-bukku**).

A: **Sumimasen, kono empitsu—anata?**
B: **Iie, watashi—ano empitsu. Sono empitsu, dōzo, anta.** A: **Dōmo.**

Tips

By now you find you can say a great
many things with very little in the way of
grammar. Just stringing the words together
with appropriate pauses is enough to convey
a lot of meaning. Japanese often talk this
way, but they also often add various elements to make the meaning clearer. We
will learn about these elements little by little.
Notice that a Japanese word has a much
wider, and vaguer, meaning than the corresponding English word. **Tabako** means
not only "cigarettes" but "a cigarette,"
"the cigarette," "some cigarettes," "a
pack of cigarettes," etc. **Anata** can mean
"you," "yours," "the one you are going to
use," etc. Of course when the Japanese wants
to be specific he has ways to narrow the meaning down, but usually he finds it unnecessary
to be too specific. Do not worry about
little English words (like *a, the, some, none,*

15

it, you, me, etc.) which often do not appear in the Japanese sentences. Japanese speakers, like Japanese artists, can achieve great effects with a few nicely poised strokes—they leave all they can to your imagination. This is part of the charm.

A: This—what (is it)? *B*: That—(it is) cigarettes. Please (have one). *A*: Thank you. (Have you) a match? *B*: Yes, please (help yourself). *A*: Thank you. *B*: Not at all. *A*: (Will it be) water? Beer? Milk? *B*: Milk. *A*: Yes sir, here you are. *B*: Thank you.

A: Say. *B*: Yeah. *A*: This—what (is it)? *B*: That—(it is) clothing. *A*: Oh? American clothes? *B*: No, Japanese clothes.

A: This book—What (is it)? *B*: That book—(it is) a textbook.

A: Excuse me, this pencil—(is it) you (it belongs to)? *B*: No, me—(the one which belongs to me, *or* the one which I am using, is) that pencil over there. That pencil (near you)—please, you (take it). *A*: Thanks.

Lesson 5

HAVE YOU GOT ANY?

PHRASES

Have you got any?	**Arimas'?** (or **Arimas'**
Have you got one?	**ka?**)
I've got some.	
I've got one.	**Arimas'.**
There is some (one).	

16

I don't have any. There isn't any.	Arimasen.
Have you got a light?	Matchi—arimas' ka?
Do you sell beer?	Biiru—arimas' ka?
Can I have some milk?	Miruku—arimas' ka?
Is there any meat?	Niku arimas' ka?
Please give me some.	Kudasai.
Give me a ticket please.	Kippu kudasai.
Hand me that book please.	Ano hon kudasai.
Pass the bread.	Pan kudasai.
Bring some vegetables.	Yasai kudasai.
Have you got any money? Is there any money?	O-kane arimas' ka?
I'm broke.	O-kane arimasen.
Give me some money.	O-kane kudasai.
Does the maid have any? Do you have a maid?	Jochū—arimas' ka?

17

Does the maid have any money?	Jochū o-kane arimas' ka?
Does the soldier have a ticket?	Heitai san — kippu arimas' ka?
Yes—that's right.	Sō des'.
a little bit	s'koshi
a lot, lots	tak'san

Practice

A: **Chotto shitsurei. Kippu arimas' ka?** B: Watashi? Watashi—kippu arimas'. Kore—kippu. A: Hai, arigato. Tomodachi—? B: Tomodachi—kippu arimasen. O-kane arimas'. A: Sō des' ka? Sumimasen. O-kane kudasai. C: Hai, dōzo. A: Sumimasen. Dōmo.

A: **Chotto, ano ne!** Waitress: Hai, hai. A: Miruku arimas' ka? W: Sumimasen. Arimasen. Biiru arimas'. O-sake arimas'. A: Sō des'ka? Biiru, o-sake, arimas'? Biiru s'koshi kudasai. W: Hai, hai.... Dōzo. A: Dōmo arigato. W: Dō itashimash'te.

A: **Chotto!** Clerk: Hai. A: Sono kimono—waf'ku? C: Sō des'. Waf'ku arimas'. Yōf'ku arimas'. A: Sore kudasai. C: Hai. Arigato gozaimas'. Dōmo.

A: **Anta—jochū arimas' ka?** B: Hai,

18

arimas'. Anta—arimas' ka ? B: Iie, arimasen. A: Jochū—waf'ku arimas' ka,
yōf'ku arimas' ka ? B: Jochū yōf'ku
arimas'. Watashi waf'ku arimas'. A: Sō
des' ka ? Watashi—waf'ku arimasen.
Yōf'ku arimas'.

TIPS

Arimas' is another word of vague meaning "there is," "we have got," "I have got,"
"you have got," etc. The little word ka at the
end of Arimas' ka ? is the question particle.
You can ask a question without it, but you
often add this particle to make the sentence
specifically a question. Another particle
often used at the end of a sentence is ne.
Arimas' ne means "there is some, you
know" or "don't you agree with me that
there is some." Sometimes the particle
makes the meaning a little softer, or more
intimate, or more sincere ; Gomen nasai ne
is just another way to say Gomen nasai
"excuse me." Words like arimas' and
kudasai usually come at the end of the sentence, and the word which comes at the end
in English often comes earlier in the Japanese sentence.

A: Excuse me, sir. Do you have a ticket? B: Me?
I've got a ticket. (Here) this is the ticket. A: Ah,
thank you. Your friend—? B: My friend—he hasn't
got a ticket. (But) he has money. A: Oh? Excuse
me. Give me money. C: OK, here (please take it).

19

A: Excuse me. Thank you.

A: Waitress, hey! *Waitress*: Yes, sir. *A*: Do you have any milk? *W*: I'm sorry, we're out of it. We have beer. We have saké. *A*: Oh? You have beer and saké? Give me a little beer. *W*: Yes, sir.... Here you are, sir. *A*: Thanks very much. *W*: Not at all.

A: Clerk! *Clerk*: Yes? *A*: That garment—(is it) Japanese? *C*: Yes, it is. We have Japanese clothes. We have American clothes. *A*: Give me that one. *C*: Yes, ma'm. Thank you. Thank you.

A: You—(do you) have a maid? *B*: Yes, I have. You—(do you) have one? *A*: No, I don't have one. Your maid—(does she) have Japanese clothes or American clothes? *B*: The maid—(she) has American clothes. Me—(I) have Japanese clothes. *A*: Oh? Me—I don't have Japanese clothes. I have American clothes.

Lesson 6

WHERE?

PHRASES

where?	**doko?**
Where is it?	**Doko?** (or **Doko des' ka?** or **Doko—arimas' ka?** or **Doko ni arimas' ka?**)
here; this place	**koko**
there; that place	**soko**
over there	**asoko** (or **as'ko**)

20

It is here.	Koko des'. (or Koko ni arimas'.)
bathroom (= toilet)	benjo
Where's the bathroom?	Benjo—doko? (or Benjo—doko des' ka?)
It is over there.	As'ko des'.
It is on the right.	Migi des'.
It is on the left.	Hidari des',
It is right ahead.	Massugu des'. (or Massugu saki des'.)
school	gakkō (or gakko)
office	jimusho
railroad station	eki
Japan	Nihon
America	Amerika
movies	eiga
theater	gekijō (or gekijo)
movie theater	eigakan
on top; above	ue (or ue ni)
below	sh'ta (or sh'ta ni)
inside	naka (or naka ni)
in front	mae (or mae ni)
in back; behind	ushiro (or ushiro ni)
ahead	saki (or saki ni)
beside, near	soba (or soba ni)
on the other side	mukō (or mukō ni)

21

PRACTICE

A: Chotto shitsurei. Benjo—doko des' ka? B: Benjo des' ka? Benjo—as'ko. Migi des'. A: Sumimasen. B: Iie.

A: Eki—doko des' ka? Koko des' ka? B: Iie, koko—gakkō des'. Eki—asoko des'. Mukō ni arimas'. A: Sō des' ka? Dōmo sumimasen. B: Dō itashimash'te.

A: Anata—eiga des' ka? ("You—is it the movies?"—This means "Are you going to the movies?" If you were talking to an actor, it could mean "Are you in the movies?") B: Hai. Sō des'. Eigakan—doko ni arimas' ka? A: Dono eigakan des' ka? Dore des' ka? B: Tōkyō Gekijō des'. A: Sō des' ka? Sore—as'ko des'. Migi, hidari, massugu saki des'. B: Ah, sō des' ka? Sore—dōmo arigato gozaimas'. Sumimasen. A: Iie. Dō itashimash'te. Shitsurei shimash'ta. Mata aimashō.

A: Anata—doko des' ka? ("You—where is it?" This could mean "Where are you going?" or "Where are you from?" or "Where do you live" or a number of other things. See if you can tell from what follows.) B: Watashi—gakkō des'. A: Sō des' ka. Sensei des' ka? B: Hai. Sō des'. Sensei

22

LESSON 6 : WHERE ?

des'. A : Gakkō—dore des' ka ? Dono gakkō des' ka ? Kono gakkō des' ka ? B : Iie, ano gakkō des'.

TIPS

The word **des'** means "is" or "it is," "I am," "you are," "he is," etc. The word **arimas'** means "there is" or "we've got some" or "he has one" or the like ; it also means "it is located." **Koko (ni) arimas'** means either "we've got it here" or "it is here." **Koko des'** means only "it is here." When the English "is" refers to location, it doesn't matter much which you use. But when the "is" tells you WHAT something is, you have to use **des'**: **Watashi—Tanaka des'**. "I'm Tanaka." **Kore—empitsu des'**. "This is a pencil." The particle **ni** means "in," "at," "to," etc.—it shows a very general sort of location or direction. With **arimas'** you can put **ni** in to help make your meaning more specific, or you can leave it out. But **ni** almost never occurs in front of **des'**. Notice that **ni**, like all particles, refers to the word in front of it (**ue ni** "ON the top," **gakkō ni** "AT the school," **doko ni** "IN what place") and is tacked right on to it when you pronounce the two words together

A : Excuse me a moment. The toilet—where is it? *B*: Is it the toilet (you want)? The toilet—(it is) over there. It's to the right. *A* : Thank you. *B*:

23

KAWASAKI READING ROOM UNL

You're welcome.

A : The railroad station—where is it? Is it here?
B : No, this place—it is a school, The station—it is
over there. It's across the way. A : Oh, I see.
Thank you very much. B : Not at all.

A : Are you going to the movies? B : Yes, I am.
The movie theater—where is it (at)? A : Which
movie house is it? B : It's Tokyo Theater. A : Oh?
That—it is over there. (It's) to the right, (then) the
left, (then) straight ahead. B : Oh, is it? Thank
you very much for (telling me) that. Thank you.
A : No, not at all. I've been rude. So long.

A : Where are you located? B : Me—(It's) a school
(I'm at). A : Oh? Are you a teacher? B : Yes,
I am. I'm a teacher. A : Your school—which one
is it? Which school is it? Is it this school? B :
No, it's that school over there.

Lesson 7

WHOSE?

Phrases

whose? (*or* of whom?)	**dare no ?**
Whose is it?	**Dare no des' ka ?**
It is mine.	**Watashi no des'.**
Is it yours?	**Anata no des' ka ?**
It is his.	**Ano hito no des'.**
What place is it of (from)?	**Doko no des' ka ?**
Is it American? (*or*	**Amerika no des' ka ?**

Is it an American one?	
It's a Japanese one.	Nihon no des'.
car (*or* taxi)	kuruma (or jidōsha)
room	heya
at home	uchi
Is your wife at home?	Ok'san—uchi des' ka?
absent	rusu
(He *or* She) is absent.	Rusu des'.
person who takes care of the house during one's absence	rusuban
Who is taking care of the house?	Rusuban—dare des' ka?
It's the one in front.	Mae no des'.
It's the one in front of the house.	Uchi no mae no des'.
It's the one in front of my house.	Watashi no uchi no mae no des'.

PRACTICE

A · Anta—doko no gakkō des' ka?
Anta no gakkō—doko no gakkō des' ka?

25

Tōkyō no des' ka, Yokohama no des' ka?
B: Tōkyō des' ne. A: Tōkyō no doko
("where in Tokyo") des' ka? Tōkyō no
Ginza des' ka? B: Iie, watashi no gakkō
—Asak'sa ni arimas'. A: Anta—Amerika-
jin no sensei des' ka? ("You—is it an
American teacher"; this can mean either
"Are you an American teacher?" or "Is
yours an American teacher?" So he goes
ahead and clarifies:) Anta no—Amerika-
jin no sensei des' ka? Anta no sensei—
Amerika-jin no sensei des' ka? Anta no
sensei — Amerika-jin des' ka? B: Iie,
watashi no sensei—Nihon-jin des'. Watashi no gakkō—Amerika-jin no sensei arimasen.

A: Kore—anta no kuruma des' ka?
B: Iie, watashi—kuruma arimasen. Kono
kuruma—Tanaka san no des'. A: Sō des'
ka. Kuruma—Tanaka san no uchi no
mae ni arimas' ka? B: Iie, watashi no
uchi no mae ni arimas'.

A: Ok'-san uchi des' ka? B: Iie, rusu
des'. A: Dare rusuban des' ka? Rusuban dare des' ka? Anta des' ka? B: Iie.
Jochū des'. Rusuban—jochū des'. Jochū
—rusuban des'. A: Sō des' ka. Watashi
jochū arimasen. Rusuban — ok'-san des'.

B: Anta no uchi—gakkō no ushiro des' ne.
A: Sō des'. Eki no mukō ni arimas'.

Tips

The particle **no** has a very general meaning "of," "belonging to," "pertaining to" (the
preceding word). **Dare no** means "whose,"
"of whom" but it also sometimes means "to
whom" or "from whom." **Gakkō no sensei** can mean "the teachers of the school"
or "the teachers in the school" or just
"the school teachers." The particle **no** is
a way to show that the preceding noun tells
something about the following noun—that
sensei is somehow connected with **gakkō**,
and **gakkō** gives you more specific information about **sensei**. It is a way of tying
down the vague and general meanings of a
Japanese noun to something more particular.
You may wonder why "teachers in the
school" doesn't have the particle **ni**; Japanese nouns can be linked to each other ONLY
by the particle **no**. The other particles (like
ni) are used when the noun is linked, not
directly with another noun, but with some
verb or a large phrase. If you wanted to
be specific about the "teachers INSIDE the
school" you would say **Gakkō no naka no
sensei**. In front of words begining with **n**,
d, or **t**, the word **nani** takes the shape **nan**;
Nan des' ka? "what is it?" **nan ni** "what
in" **nan no shita ni** "under what."

27

A: What school are you at? What school is your school? Is it (one) in Tokyo, or is it (one) in Yokohama? *B*: It's (in) Tokyo. *A*: Whereabouts in Tokyo is it? Is it in Tokyo's Ginza (area)? *B*: No, my school is in Asakusa. *A*: Is your teacher American? Is yours an American teacher? Is your teacher an American teacher? Is your teacher an American? *B*: No, my teacher is a Japanese. (In) my school—we have no American teachers.

A: This—is it your car? *B*: No, me—(I) haven't got a car. This car—it's Mr. Tanaka's. *A*: Oh, is it? Is the car (parked) in front of Mr. Tanaka's house? *B*: No, it is (parked) in front of my house.

A: Is your wife (at) home? *B*: No, she's out. *A*: Who's taking care of the place? Who's the one taking care of the house? Is it you? *B*: No. It's the maid. The one taking care of the house is the maid. The maid is the one taking care of the house. *A*: Oh, is it? I haven't got a maid. The one who takes care of my house when I'm away is my wife. *B*: Your house is back of the school, isn't it. *A*: That's right. It's across from the railroad station.

Lesson 8

WHEN ?

PHRASES

when?	**itsu ?**
When is it? (o*r* When will it be?)	**Itsu des' ka ?**
When was it?	**Itsu desh'ta ka ?**
today	**kyō**
yesterday	**kinō**

tomorrow	ash'ta
tonight	komban
tomorrow night	ash'ta no ban (or myōban)
last night	kinō no ban (or sakuban or yūbe)
now	ima
soon	ma-mo-naku (or hayaku)
right away	sugu (or hayaku)
fast (or quickly)	hayaku
later, later on	ato (or ato de)
before (hand)	mae (or mae ni)
It was last year.	Kyonen desh'ta.
this year	kotoshi
next year	rainen
well (or Well, now let me see.)	Sō des' ne... or Sā... or Ē-to... or Ē...
well, I guess...	mā
oh my goodness !	mā! (or yā !)
already	mō
It's already done.	Mō shimash'ta.
I did it.	Watashi—shimash'ta.
Who did it ?	Dare shimash'ta ? (or Dare shimash'ta ka ?)
I have been rude.	Shitsure(i) shimash'ta.
not yet	mada (or Mada des'.)

29

PRACTICE

A : Anta — Kōbe—itsu des' ka? B:
Ash'ta des'. Ash'ta no ban des'. A: Sō
des' ka. Kōbe no doko des' ka? B: As'-
ko no tomodachi no uchi des'. Sono uchi
—eki no soba des'. Anta—Kōbe—kyonen
desh'ta ne. A: Iie. Mada des'.

Tanaka: Moshi moshi, Nakamura san!
N: Hai, nan des' ka? Dare des' ka?
Anta des' ka, Tanaka san? Konnichi wa.
T: Konnichi wa, Nakamura san. Anta—
doko des' ka? N: Tōkyō des'. Tōkyō-eki
no mukō no Marunouchi *Building* des'.
T: Sō des' ka. Watashi—ima Ginza des':
ato de Kanda des' ne.

Conductor: Sumimasen. Kippu arimas'
ka? N: Hai, dōzo. C: Arigato. Dōmo...
Shimbashi, Shimbashi des'! Ma-mo-naku
Tōkyō des'. T: Mā! Mō Tōkyō des' ne.
Sugu sayonara des' ne. N: Sō des' ne.
Sā, mata aimashō ne. C: Tōkyo, Tōkyō
des'! Tōkyō-eki des'. T: Sayonara. N:
Sayonara. Shitsurei shimash'ta.

A : Anta no gakkō — itsu des' ka?
("Your school—when is it": this could mean
"When does your school take up?" "When
does your school let out?" "When is it
time for your school to do something?"

30

"When do you go away to school?" etc. depending on the situation) B: Sō des' ne. Mä, rainen des' ne. A: Sō des' ka. Watashi no gakkō—ma-mo-naku ne. Anta no gakkō—ato des' ne.

TIPS

The Japanese puts his family name before his personal name. So Mr. Tanaka's son Tarō calls himself Tanaka Tarō and other people call him Tanaka Taro san. You add san "Mr.," "Mrs.," "Miss" to the name if it is someone else; but you never use it of yourself: Anta Tanaka san des' ka? Hai. watashi — Tanaka des'. Many Japanese name their first son Ichirō, the second Jirō, the third Saburō, and the fourth Shirō. Other men's personal names often end in -o, -shi, or -u (Yoshio, Hiroshi, Susumu). Many girl's names end in -ko (Hanako, Haruko, Fumiko); some end in -e (Shizue, Harue, Fumie), or in -yo (Haruyo, Miyo, Chiyo). The word sense(i) by itself means "teacher"; as a title it is used like "Dr." —as a term of respect for physicians, teachers, and other learned professions. The word for "Reverend" is bokushi or bokushi san; by itself it means "preacher." Catholic priests are called shimpu or shimpu san. Notice that Japanese who adopt American names tend to give the name in American order Tonii Tani san, not Tani Tonii

31

san. It will be less confusing if you do not reverse your name as if it were Japanese: John Smith (**san**), not Smith John (**san**).

A: You, Kobe, when is it? (When are you going to Kobe?) *B*: It's tomorrow. It's tomorrow night. *A*: It is? Where in Kobe will it be (that you'll be staying)? *B*: It will be the house of a friend there. His house is right near the station. You were in Kobe last year, weren't you. *A*: No, I have yet to go.

Tanaka: Hey there, Mr. Nakamura! *N*: Yes, what is it? Who is it? Is it you, Mr. Tanaka? Hello. *T*: Hello, Mr. Nakamura. Where are you headed? *N*: I'm headed for Tokyo Station. I'm going to the Marunouchi Building across from Tokyo Station. *T*: Oh? Me—right now (I'm) on my way to the Ginza; later (I'm) going to Kanda.

Conductor: Excuse me. Do you have a ticket? *N*: Yes, here it is. *C*: Thank you. Thank you... Shimbashi, it's Shimbashi! Soon it will be Tokyo (Station). *T*: My goodness. We're already in Tokyo. We'll soon be saying goodbye. *N*: So we will. Well, see you again, huh? *C*: Tokyo, it's Tokyo. It's Tokyo Station. *T*: Goodbye. *N*: Goodbye. I've been rude.

A: When is it your school begins? *B*: Let me see, why, it's after the first of the year (into the next calendar year). *B*: Is that so? My school begins soon. Your school is later, isn't it.

Lesson 9

HOW MUCH?

PHRASES

how much?	ikura?
How much is it?	Ikura des' ka?
1 Yen	ichi en
5 Yen	go en
10 Yen (¥10)	jū en
20 Yen	ni-jū en (or futa-jū en)
30 Yen	san-jū en
40 Yen	yon-jū en (or shi-jū en)
50 Yen	go-jū en
60 Yen	roku-jū en
70 Yen	nana-jū en (or shichi-jū en)
80 Yen	hachi-jū en
90 Yen	kyū-jū en
100 Yen	hyaku en
200 Yen	ni-hyaku en (or futa-hyaku en)
250 Yen	ni-hyaku go-jū en
300 Yen	sam-byaku en
400 Yen	yon-hyaku en
500 Yen	go-hyaku en

33

600 Yen	**rop-pyaku en** (or **roku-hyaku en**)
700 Yen	**nana-hyaku en**
800 Yen	**hap-pyaku en** (or **hachi-hyaku en**)
900 Yen	**kyū-hyaku en** (or **ku-hyaku en**)
1000 Yen	**sen en**
2000 Yen	**ni-sen en**
3000 Yen	**san-zen en**
4000 Yen	**yon-sen en**
10,000 Yen	**ichi-man en**
20,000 Yen	**ni-man en**
1 million Yen	**hyaku-man en**
high, expensive	**takai**
cheap	**yasui**

PRACTICE

A: **Chotto ne.** Clerk: **Hai.** A: **Kore— ikura des' ka?** C: **Sō des' ne. Sore— ni-hyaku en des'.** A: **Sō des' ka? Ni- hyaku en des' ka? Are—ikura des' ka?** C: **Kore des' ka? Kore—hyaku go-jū en des'.** A: **Sore kudasai.** C: **Hai, arigato gozaimas'. Go-hyaku en des' ka? Chotto matte kudasai....Sumimasen. Kore—sam- byaku go-jū en des'. Dōmo arigato.** A: **Iie. Sayonara.** C: **Sayonara.**

A: **Ano hon—anta no des' ka, Tanaka**

34

san? T: Kore des' ka? Kono hon des'
ka? Hai, watashi no des'. A: Ikura
desh'ta ka—sono hon? T: Sō des' ne.
Ikura desh'ta ka ne. Chotto matte kudasai. Hanako, Hanako! Wife: Hai, hai,
Nan desh'ta ka? T: Kono hon des' ne—
ikura desh'ta ka? Wife: Ē, ni-hyaku
go-jū en desh'ta ne. A: Sō des' ka. Tanaka san no ok'-san, dōmo sumimasen.
Wife: Dō itashimash'te. Shitsurei shimash'ta. T: Kanai—shitsurei shimash'-
ta. (he is apologizing to the guest for his
wife's intrusion.) A: Iie, watashi—shitsurei shimash'ta.

A: Watashi—eiga des'. (" I'm off for
the movies.") Anta—eiga des' ka? B: Sō
des' ne. Anta—doko no eiga des' ka?
A: Nichi-geki (Nihon Gekijō) des'. B:
Sō des' ka. Sono eigakan no kippu—ikura
des' ka. A: Sō des' ne. Sā, ni-hyaku en
des' ne. B: Takai des' ne—sore. Yasui
kippu no eigakan—arimasen ka? Yasui
eigakan arimasen ka? A: Arimas'. Eki
no soba ni, yasui eigakan arimas'. B:
Sono eki no soba no eigakan no kippu—
yasui des' ka? Ikura des' ka? A: Kippu
—hachi-jū en. Sore—yasui ne. B: Hai,
yasui des'. Watashi—sono eigakan des'.
Anta? A: Hai, watashi—sono yasui eiga-

35

kan. A : **Anta—okane tak'san arimas'
ka?** B : **Iie, tak'san arimasen. S'koshi
arimas' ne.** A : **Ikura arimas' ka?** B : **Sō
des' ne. Ni-hyaku en arimas'.**

TIPS

Money is counted in Yen. There are bills
for ¥100 (**hyaku-en satsu**), ¥500 (**go-
hyaku-en satsu**), ¥1000 (**sen-en satsu**), and
¥5000 (**go-sen-en satsu**). There is a ¥1
coin (**ichi-en-dama**), a perforated ¥5 brass
coin (**go-en-dama**), a solid ¥10 copper coin
(**jū-en-dama**), a ¥50 coin (**gojū-en-dama**),
and a ¥100 coin (**hyaku-en-dama**).

A : Excuse me. *Clerk* : Yes sir. *A* : How much
is this? *C* : Let me see. That is 200 Yen. *A* : Oh?
It's 200 Yen? That over there, how much is it?
C : You mean this one? This is 150 Yen. *A* : I'll
take that one. *C* : Yes sir, thank you. Is it 500 Yen
(you are handing me)? Yes? Excuse me a minute....
Sorry. Here (this is)—350 Yen (change). Thank
you very much. *A* : You're welcome. Goodbye.
C : Goodbye.

A : Is that book yours, Mr. Tanaka? *T* : You
mean this one? Is it this book (you mean)? Yes, it
is mine. *A* : How much was it, that book? *T* : Let
me see. How much was it now.... Wait just a minute. Hanako, Hanako! *Wife* : Yes, yes. What
was it (you wanted)? *T* : This book, you know—
how much was it? *Wife* : Why, it was 250 Yen.
A : Oh really? Thank you, Mrs. Tanaka. *Wife* :
Not at all. I've been rude. *T* : My wife was rude.
A : Not at all, it was rude of me.

A : I'm going to the movies. Are you going to the
movies? *B* : Well, let's see. Which movie are you
going to? *A* : The one at the Nichigeki. *B* : Oh?

How much are the tickets at that theater ? *A*: Let me think, why they are 200 Yen. *B*: That's expensive, isn't it. Isn't there a theater with cheaper tickets? Isn't there a cheaper theater? *A*: Yes, there is. There is a cheap movie next to the railroad station. *B*: Are the tickets cheap to that theater by the station? How much are they? *A*: The tickets are 80 Yen. That's cheap, isn't it. *B*: Yes, that's cheap. I'm for that theater. How about you? *A*: Yes, I'll go to that cheap theater. *A*: Do you have lots of money (with you)? *B*: No, I don't have lots. I have a little. *A*: How much do you have? *B*: Let me see. I have 200 Yen.

Lesson 10

HOW MANY ? HOW OLD ?

PHRASES

how many? (*or* how many years old?)	ikutsu ?
1	hitotsu
2	f'tatsu
3	mittsu
4	yottsu
5	itsutsu
6	muttsu
7	nanatsu
8	yattsu
9	kokonotsu
10	tō

37

11	jū ichi
12	jū ni
20	ni-jū
30	san-jū
100	hyaku
102	hyaku ni
one more	mō hitotsu
child, son	kodomo
daughter, girl	musume, musume san

PRACTICE

A: Tanaka san, anta no kodomo—ikutsu des' ka? T: Muttsu des'. Mō gakkō des'. A: Sō des' ka? Watashi no kodomo—yottsu des'. Gakko—mada des'. A: Anta no uchi no naka ni—tēburu arimas' ka? B: Hai, tak'san arimas'. A: Sō des' ka? Ikutsu arimas' ka? B: Itsutsu arimas'. A: Itsutsu arimas' ka? Watashi—f'tatsu arimas'. Anta—okane tak'san arimas' ka? A: Iie, tak'san arimasen. O-kane tak'san arimasen. Tēburu tak'san arimas' ne.

A: *Hotel* no soba ni eigakan arimas' ka? B: Hai, f'tatsu mittsu ("2 or 3") arimas' ne. Hitotsu—Amerika no eiga des'. F'tatsu—Nihon no eiga des'. A: Sō des' ka? Kippu—takai des' ka? A: Amerika no eiga no kippu—s'koshi takai des'.

38

Nihon no eiga no kippu—s'koshi yasuî des'.

A : **Biiru hitotsu kudasai.** Waitress:
**Hai, hai. Biiru des' ka? Biiru mittsu
arimas'. Hitotsu—Nippon Biiru, mō hitotsu—Kirin Biiru, mō hitotsu—Asahi
Biiru des'.** A: **Sō des' ka. Amerika no
biiru—arimasen ka?** W: **Arimasen ne.
Nihon no biiru des'.** A: *Juice* ("orange
pop")** arimas' ka?** W: **Arimas'.** A: **Sore
hitotsu kudasai.** W: **Hai, hai.**

TIPS

All sorts of objects are counted with the
series **hitotsu, f'tatsu,** etc., but only up
to 10; above that the numbers are the same
that you have learned to count money with:
1 **ichi,** 2 **ni,** 3 **san,** 4 **yon** or **shi,** 5 **go,**
6 **roku,** 7 **nana** or **shichi,** 8 **hachi,** 9 **kyū**
or **ku,** 10 **jū,** etc. Notice that 15 is made
by saying "ten-five" (**jū go**), and 50 by
saying "five-ten" (**go-jū**). There are some
objects which are customarily counted in
some special way; for example, long, slender
objects (pencils, cigarettes, bottles of beer,
etc.) are counted **ip-pon, ni-hon, sam-bon,
yon-hon, go-hon, roku-hon** or **rop-pon,
nana-hon, hachi-hon** or **hap-pon, kyū-hon,
jip-pon** or **jū-hon.** But if you forget, you
will be understood if you say **empitsu f'-
tatsu** instead of **empitsu ni-hon** "2 pen-

39

cils." **Biiru hitotsu** means "one beer" and **biiru ip-pon** means "a bottle of beer," but they usually turn out to be the same thing. Flat objects (newspapers, tickets, cloths, currency bills, etc.) are counted with **-mai: shimbun ichi-mai** "one newspaper," **kippu ni-mai** "2 tickets," **sen-en-satsu sam-mai** "3 ¥1000-bills." It doesn't matter whether you put the number before or after the noun it is counting, but it comes after the noun more often, as do **tak'san** "lots" and **s'koshi**. You can say **S'koshi okane arimas'**, but it usually sounds better if you say **Okane s'koshi arimas'**.

  A : Mr. Tanaka, how old is your boy? *T*: He's 6. He's already in school. *A*: Really? My boy is 4. He's not in school yet. *A*: Do you have tables in your house? *B*: Sure, lots of them. *A*: Oh? How many have you got? *B*: We've got 5. *A*: You've got 5? Me—I've got 2. Do you have lots of money? *A*: No, I don't have lots. I haven't got lots of money. It's tables I've got a lot of.

  A : Is there a theater right near the hotel? *B*: Yes, there are 2 or 3. One shows American pictures. Two show Japanese pictures. *A*: Oh? Are the tickets expensive? *B*: The tickets for the American movies are a bit high. The tickets to the Japanese movies are rather cheap.

  A : Bring me a beer please. *Waitress.* Yes sir: It's beer (you want)? We have three (kinds of) beer. One is Nippon Beer, another is Kirin Beer, and the third is Asahi Beer. *A*: Oh? You haven't got any American beer? *W*: No, we haven't. It's Japanese beer (we serve). *A*: Do you have orange pop? *W*: Yes, we do. *A*: Let me have one of those. *W*: Yes, sir.

40

Lesson 11

HOW MANY PEOPLE?

PHRASES

how many people?	**nan-nin?**
1 person (*or* alone)	**hitori**
2 people	**f'tari**
3 people	**san-nin**
4 people	**yo-nin**
5 people	**go-nin**
6 people	**roku-nin**
7 people	**nana-nin**
8 people	**hachi-nin**
9 people	**ku-nin**
10 people	**jū-nin**
11 people	**jū-ichi-nin**
100 people	**hyaku-nin**
people, other people, a person	**hito**
cousin	**itoko**
brothers and sisters	**kyōdai**
brother(s)	**otoko no kyōdai**
sister(s)	**onna no kyōdai**
man (male)	**otoko**

41

woman	onna
big brother	ani (or nii-san)
big sister	ane (or nē-san)
little brother	otōto
little sister	imōto
all	minna
name	namae

PRACTICE

A: Anata—kyōdai nan-nin arimas' ka?
B: Watashi des' ka? Watashi—go-nin
arimas'. Watashi no kyōdai go-nin des'.
A: Sō des' ka. Minna otoko no kyōdai
des' ka? B: Iie. F'tari—otoko des'. San-
nin—onna des'. A: Otoko no kyōdai—
f'tari—nii-san des' ka? B: Iie. Hitori—
ani des'. Mō hitori—otōto des'. A: Otōto
san—ikutsu des' ka? B: Ni-jū san des'.
Watashi—ni-jū roku des'. A: Onna no
kyōdai—minna imōto san des' ka? B:
Iie, f'tari—imōto, mō hitori—ane des'.
A: Nē-san mō ok'-san des'ka? Danna san
arimas' ka? B: Hai, sō des'. Shujin
arimas'. Ok'san des'. A: Kodomo arimas' ka? Nan-nin arimas' ka? B: Arimas'. Hitori arimas'. Otoko des'. Sono
kodomo no namae—Tarō des'. A: Anta—
kodomo arimas' ne. B: Hai, sō des'. Onna
des'. Namae—Hanako des'. A: Sō des'

42

ka. Mā, Tarō, Hanako—itoko des' ne.
B: Sō des'. Tarō—itoko hitori arimas'.
Hanako—itoko hitori arimas'. Kodomo
f'tari—itoko f'tari des' ne. Anta—itoko
tak'san arimas' ka? B: Yonin arimas'.
Hitori—Amerika des'. Mō san-nin minna
Nihon des'.

Sensei: Kono gakkō no naka ni heya
ikutsu arimas' ka? Gak'sei: Tak'san
arimas' ne. Hitotsu, f'tatsu, mittsu, yottsu, itsutsu, muttsu, nanatsu—nanatsu
arimas' ne. Sensei: Kono heya no naka
ni hito nan-nin arimas' ka? ("How many
people have we got in this room?"—there is
another way to say "How many are in this
room?" with the verb imas' "stays.")
Gak'sei: Sō des' ne. Sensei—hitori, watashi f'tari, Tanaka san—san-nin, Nakamura san—yo-nin, Nakamura san no otōto
san—go-nin; sā, gonin des' ne. Sensei:
Minna' anata no tomodachi des' ka? Gak'-
sei: Sō des'. Minna tomodachi des'. Gakkō no tomodachi des'.

TIPS

People are counted a bit irregularly. But
it would be confusing to resort to hitotsu,
f'tatsu, etc. in counting them. Notice that
ikutsu when it refers to people can mean

only " how old "—so **kodomo f'tatsu des'**
can only mean " the boy is two," not " it's
two boys." The latter has to be **kodomo
f'tari des'**.

A : How many brothers and sisters do you have?
B : Me? I have 5. My brothers and sisters are 5
in number. *A* : Oh? Are they all brothers? *B* :
No. Two are brothers, two are sisters. *A* : Your
brothers—are they both older than you? *B* : No.
One is an older brother. The other is a younger
brother. *A* : How old is the younger brother? *B* :
He's 23. Me—I'm 26. *A* : Your sisters—are they
all younger than you? *B* : No. Two of them are
younger, the other one is older. *A* : Is your older
sister already married (" a wife ")? Has she got a
husband? *B* : Yes, she has. She's got a husband. She's married. *A* : Has she got any children? How many has she got? *B* : Yes, she has.
She has one. It's a boy. The boy's name is Taro.
A : You have a child too, don't you. *B* : That's
right. It's a girl. Her name is Hanako. *A* : Is that
right? Why, Taro and Hanako—they are cousins,
aren't they. *B* : That's right. Taro has a cousin.
Hanako has a cousin. The two children are both
cousins. Do you have lots of cousins? *B* : I've got
4. One is in America. The other 3 are all in Japan.

Teacher : How many rooms are there in this
school? *Student* : There are a lot, aren't there. 1, 2,
3, 4, 5, 6, 7—there are 7. *Teacher* : How many people
have we got in this room? *Student* : Let's see now.
Teacher is one, I'm two, Mr. Tanaka is 3, Mr. Nakamura is 4, Mr. Nakamura's little brother is 5;
why, it's 5 people (we've got). *Teacher* : Are they
all your friends? *Student* : Yes. They are all friends
(of mine). They are school friends.

44

Lesson 12
WHAT TIME?

Phrases

what time?	**nan-ji?**
What time is it?	**Nan-ji des' ka?**
1 o'clock	**ichi-ji**
2 o'clock	**ni-ji**
3 o'clock	**san-ji**
4 o'clock	**yo-ji**
5 o'clock	**go-ji**
6 o'clock	**roku-ji**
7 o'clock	**nana-ji** (or **shichi-ji**)
8 o'clock	**hachi-ji**
9 o'clock	**ku-ji**
10 o'clock	**jū-ji**
11 o'clock	**jū-ichi-ji**
12 o'clock	**jū-ni-ji**
morning (A.M.)	**asa** (or **gozen**)
mid-day	**hiru**
afternoon (P.M.)	**hiru kara** (or **gogo**)
evening	**ban**
8 A.M.	**gozen hachi-ji**
3 P.M.	**gogo san-ji**
7 in the evening	**ban no nana-ji**

...and a half	...han
5:30 P.M.	gogo go-ji han
1 minute	ip-pun
2 minutes	ni-fun
3 minutes	sam-pun
4 minutes	yon-pun
5 minutes	go-fun
6 minutes	roku-fun (or rop-pun)
7 minutes	nana-fun
8 minutes	hachi-fun (or hap-pun)
9 minutes	kyū-fun
10 minutes	jip-pun
4:25 P.M.	gogo yo-ji ni-jū go-fun
10 minutes before 3	san-ji jip-pun mae
10 minutes after 3	san-ji jip-pun (or san-ji jip-pun sugi)
watch, clock	tokei

PRACTICE

A: Chotto sumimasen. Ima nan-ji des'
ka? B: Sō des' ne. Chotto matte. Tokei
arimas'. Sā, ima yo-ji han des' ne. A:
Ah, sō des' ka? Yo-ji han des' ka? Dōmo, sore, sumimasen. B: Iie. Dō itashimash'te. Sayonara. A: Sayonara. Shitsurei shimash'ta.

A: Anta—tokei arimas' ka? Ima nan-
ji des' ka? B: Ima san-ji des' ne. A:

Arigato. Komban no eiga—nan-ji des'
ka? B: Sō des' ne. Shimbun arimas' ka?
A: Hai, arimas'. B: Doko ni arimas' ka?
A: Tēburu no ue ni arimasen ka? B:
Arimasen, tēburu no ue ni. Tēburu no
shita des' ka? A: Iie, iie. Koko ni
arimas'. Watashi no hon no shita ni
arimas'. Dōzo. B: Dono eigakan des' ka?
Eigakan—dore des' ka? A: Tōkyō Gekijō
des' ne. B: Ah, sō des' ka? Tōkyō
Gekijō... sō des' ne... ah, koko des'. Sore
—gogo roku-ji han des'. Kore—kyō no
shimbun des' ka? B: Iie, kinō no des'.
Sakuban no des'. A: Kyō no—arimas'
ka? B: Arimas'. Dōzo. B: Hai, dōmo.

A: Gakkō—nanji des' ka. B: Asa
hachi-ji han des'. A: Hiru kara—gakkō
des' ka? B: Iie, hiru kara shigoto
("work") des'. Arubaito ("job on the
side") des'. Sono shigoto—gak'sei-aru-
baito des'. Watashi—arubaito-gak'sei
des'. A: Anta no arubaito—doko des' ka?
Doko—arubaito shimas' ka? B: Jimusho
no shigoto des'. Eki no mukō no jimusho des'. As'ko—watashi arubaito shimas'. A: Sono shigoto—nan-ji des' ka?
B: Gogo ni-ji jū-go-fun mae des'.

47

TIPS

If you get confused with Japanese numbers, use your fingers, or write the figures down. Notice how Japanese count by bending the fingers of one hand—the thumb in the palm is one, then each of the fingers bent over the thumb in order (2, 3, 4, 5); from 6 to 10, the fingers are unbent in reverse order—the little finger popping back up is six, and so on to the thumb, which is 10. Japanese children learn their arithmetic using an abacus or counting-beads (**soroban**), and shopkeepers sometimes will show you the count on the abacus instead of saying the total.

A: Excuse me a moment. What time is it now? *B*: Let me see. Wait a minute. I've got a watch. Why, it is half past four (now). *A*: Oh, it is? It's half past four? Thanks, that (was very nice of you), thank you very much. *B*: Not at all, think nothing of it. Goodbye. *A*: Goodbye. I've been rude.

A: Do you have a watch? What time is it (now)? *B*: (Now) it is 3 o'clock. *A*: Thank you. What time is tonight's movie? *B*: Let me see now. Have you got a newspaper? *A*: Yes, I've got one. *B*: Where is it? *A*: Isn't it on top of the table? *B*: No, it isn't, not on top of the table. Is it underneath the table? *A*: No, no. Here it is. It's under my book. Here (please take it). *B*: Which movie house is it? The movie house—which one is it? *A*: It's Tokyo Theater. *B*: Oh? Tokyo Theater... now let me see... ah, here it is. That—it's 6:30 P.M. Is this today's paper? *B*: No, it's yesterday's. It's last night's. *A*: Do you have today's? *B*: Yes, I do. Here it is (please take it). *B*: Thank you.

48

A: What time is school ? *B*: It's at 8 : 30 in the morning. *A*: Is there school in the afternoon *B*: No, in the afternoon I work. It's a part-time job on the side. The job is a student-sideline. I'm a self-supporting ("sideline-job") student. *A*: Where is your extra job ? Where do you do your sideline work ? *B*: It's office work. It's an office across from the station. That place—(that's where) I do my sideline work. *A*: What time is your job there ? *B*: It's at a quarter before 2 P.M.

Lesson 13

HOW LONG ?

PHRASES

how many hours ? how long ?	**nan-jikan ?**
How many hours is it ?	**Nan-jikan des' ka ?**
It is 3 hours.	**San-jikan des'.**
How long does it take ?	**Nan-jikan kakarimas' ka ?**
It takes 4 hours and a half.	**Yo-jikan han kakarimas'.**
how many weeks ?	**nan-shūkan ?**
1 week	**is-shūkan**
2 weeks	**ni-shūkan**
3 weeks	**san-shūkan**
how many months?	**nan-kagetsu ?**

49

1 month	ik-kagetsu
2 months	ni-kagetsu
6 months	rok-kagetsu
8 months	hak-kagetsu
10 months	jik-kagetsu
what month?	nan-gatsu?
January	Ichi-gatsu (or Shōgatsu)
February	Ni-gatsu
March	San-gatsu
April	Shi-gatsu
May	Go-gatsu
June	Roku-gatsu
July	Shichi-gatsu
August	Hachi-gatsu
September	Ku-gatsu
October	Jū-gatsu
November	Jū-ichi-gatsu
December	Jū-ni-gatsu
last month	sengetsu
this month	kongetsu
next month	raigetsu
last week	senshū
this week	konshū
next week	raishū
how many years?	nan-nen?
(*or* what year?)	
one year (*or* the year 1)	ichi-nen

4 years (or the   **yo-nen**
year 4)
1957 ('57)   **sen kyū-hyaku go-jū**
          nana-nen   (go-jū
          nana-nen)

PRACTICE

A: Koko—as'ko—nan-jikan kakarimas'
ka ?   B: Sō des' ne. Yo-jikan han kakarimas'.

A: Chotto sumimasen. Tōkyō—Kamakura—nan-jikan des' ka ?   B: Kamakura
des' ka ?   Kamakura—ichi-jikan kakarimas'.   A: Sō des' ka ?   Ichi-jikan des' ka ?
Ichi-jikan kakarimas' ka ?   Dōmo arigato
gozaimas'.   B: Dō itashimashite.

Sensei: Ichi-nen ni—nan-kagetsu arimas'
ka ?   Gak'sei: Jū-ni-kagetsu arimas' ne.
S: Sō des'.   Ichi-nen—jū-ni-kagetsu des'.
Ik-kagetsu ni—nan-shūkan arimas' ka ?
G: Yon-shūkan des'.   S: Sō des, sō des'.
Ik-kagetsu—yon-shūkan des' ne.   Ima
nan-gatsu des' ka ?   G: Ima Jū-gatsu
des'.   S: Nan-nen des' ka, ima.   G: Sō
des' ne.   Go-jū roku-nen des' ne.   Sen
kyū-hyaku go-jū roku-nen des' ne.   S: Sō
des'.   Go-jū roku-nen no Jū-gatsu des' ne.
Sengetsu—nan-gatsu desh'ta ka ?   G: Kugatsu desh'ta.   Raigetsu—Jū-ichi-gatsu

des' ne. S: Sō des'. Kongetsu—Jū-gatsu des' ne. Kyonen—nan-nen desh'ta ka? G: Go-jū go-nen desh'ta. S: Rainen? G: Rainen—gojū nana-nen des' ne. S: Sō des' ne. Dōmo sumimasen desh'ta. G: Dō itashimash'te. Shitsurei shimash'ta.

TIPS

Do not confuse **-ji** " o'clock " with **-jikan** "hour." **Jikan** by itself means "time": **Jikan arimas' ka?** "Is there time (enough)?" **Jikan des'** "It's time (class is over, etc.)." **Mō jikan des' ka?** "Is the time up?" Do not confuse the **-gatsu** of the month names with **-kagetsu** (counting months), or **-getsu** (in **sen-getsu** "last month," etc.).

NOTE

Days are counted quite irregularly from 1 to 10, but you will be understood if you count them according to the pattern **ichi-nichi, ni-nichi, san-nichi, yon-nichi, go-nichi,** etc. If you want to say October 10th, say **Jū-gatsu ju-nichi** or **Jū-gatsu no jū-nichi.** The word for "day" by itself is **hi: Sono hi—nan-nichi desh'ta ka?** "What date was that day?"

A: (From) here—(to) there—how many hours does it take? *B:* Let me think...It takes 4 and a half hours.

A : Excuse me, sir. (From) Tokyo—(to) Kamakura—how many hours is it? *B* : Kamakura? Kamakura—it takes an hour. *A* : It does? It's an hour? It takes an hour? Thank you very much. *B* : Not at all.

Teacher : How many months are there in a year? *Student* : There are 12 (months). *Teacher* : That's right. A year is 12 months. How many weeks are there in a month? *Student* : There are four weeks. Teacher : That's right, that's right. One month is four weeks. What month is this (is it now)? *Student* : This (now) is October. *Teacher* : What year is this (is it now)? *Student* : Let me see. It's '56. It's 1956. *Teacher* : That's right. It's October '56. What month was last month? *Student* : It was September. Next month will be November, won't it. *Teacher* : That's right. This month is October, isn't it. What year was last year? *Student* : It was '55. *Teacher* : Next year? *Student* : Next year is '57. *Teacher* : So it is, isn't it. Thank you very much. *Student* : Not at all. I've been rude.

ADDED NOTE

If you wish to learn the more usual way to count days, study the following table :

1. tsui-tachi	6. mui-ka
2. futsu-ka	7. nano-ka
3. mik-ka	8. yō-ka
4. yok-ka	9. kokono-ka
5. itsu-ka	10. tō-ka

(This table can be nicely sung to the theme of Haydn's Surprise Symphony.)

PART II

Add a Bit of Action

Lesson 14

DID YOU?

PHRASES

Did you do it?	**Shimash'ta ka?**
Did you see the movie?	**Eiga mimash'ta ka?**
I saw it.	**Mimash'ta.**
I didn't see it.	**Mimasen desh'ta.**
Did your friend come?	**Tomodachi kimash'ta ka?**
He came.	**Kimash'ta.**
He didn't come.	**Kimasen desh'ta.**
Where'd the teacher go?	**Sensei doko ikimash'ta ka?**
He went home.	**Kaerimash'ta.**
food (or meal or cooked rice)	**gohan**
food (something to eat)	**tabemono**
meal	**shokuji**
Have you eaten (your meal)?	**Gohan tabemash'ta ka?**
I have eaten already.	**Mō tabemash'ta.**
I haven't eaten yet.	**Mada tabemasen.**

Did you read the book?	**Hon yomimash'ta ka?**
Did you write a letter?	**Tegami kakimash'ta ka?**
Did you drink beer?	**Biiru nomimash'ta ka?**
Did you buy the tickets?	**Kippu kaimash'ta ka?**
Did you sell the car?	**Kuruma urimash'ta ka?**
Did you ask the policeman?	**Omawari-san ni kikimash'ta ka?**
Did you listen to the radio?	**Rajio kikimash'ta ka?**
Did you watch television?	**Terebi mimash'ta ka?**
Did you meet (see) any people?	**Hito ni aimash'ta ka?**
Did you talk Japanese?	**Nihongo—hanashimash'ta ka?**
English	**Eigo**
Did you say that?	**Sō iimash'ta ka?**
I didn't say that.	**Sō iimasen desh'ta.**
Did you do like that? (or Did you do that?)	**Sō shimash'ta ka?**
Did you study hard? (or a lot or well)	**Yoku benkyō shimash'ta ka?**

Practice

A: Anata, sakuban, nani shimash'ta ka?
Eigakan ikimash'ta ka? B: Iie, sakuban,
uchi desh'ta. Terebi mimash'ta. A: Sō
des' ka? Terebi itsu kaimash'ta ka? B:
Sengetsu kaimash'ta. A: Takai desh'ta
ka. B: Sō des' ne. S'koshi takai desh'ta
ne. Jū man en desh'ta. A: Takaı ne,
sore. B: Anta, sakuban, eiga desh'ta ka?
A: Iie, Ginza ikimash'ta. Sh'kashi
("But") eiga mimasen desh'ta. Gohan
tabemash'ta. B: Sō des' ka? Ginza de
gohan tabemash'ta ka? Ginza no res'-
toran ("restaurant") takai des'ne. A: Sō
des'. Keredomo ("though") watashi—yasui
res'toran desh'ta. Gohan—yasui desh'ta.
Biiru nomimasen desh'ta. B: Biiru nomimasen desh'ta ka? Nani nomimash'ta
ka? A: Ocha nomimash'ta. Biiru takai
des'. Ocha yasui des'. B: Ato de, nani
shimash'ta ka, anta? Hito ni aimash'ta
ka? A: Iie, ato de hito ni aimasen
desh'ta. Hayaku kaerimash'ta. Benkyō shimash'ta. B: Nan no benkyō shimash'ta ka? Dono benkyō shimash'ta
ka? Eigo no benkyō desh'ta ka? A: Iie,
Eigo no benkyō shimasen desh'ta. Nihongo
benkyō shimash'ta. Nihongo no benkyō
desh'ta. Nihongo no benkyō shimash'ta.

B: **Yoku benkyō shimash'ta ka?** Nan-jikan desh'ta ka? A: **Yo-jikan benkyō shimash'ta.** B: **Ok'-san—benkyō desh'ta ka? Ok'-san—benkyō shimash'ta ka, saku-ban.** A: **Iie, tegami kakimash'ta. Sore kara** ("after that"), **hon yomimash'ta.**

TIPS

Verbs in the polite past ("some one did something." "Did someone do something?") have the ending **-mash'ta**; if they are negative ("Someone did not do something." "Didn't someone do something?") the ending is **-masen desh'ta.** The word **desh'ta** by itself (following a noun or adjective) means "was": **Kyonen desh'ta** "It was last year," **Yasui desh'ta** "It was cheap." Notice that the subject is often omitted in Japanese— you have to guess from the situation.

A: What did you do last night? Did you go to the movies? *B:* No, last night, I was at home. I watched television. *A:* You did? When did you buy a television set? *B:* I bought one last month. *A:* Was it expensive? *B:* Well... it was a bit expensive, all right. It was 100,000 Yen. *A:* That is expensive, isn't it, that. *B:* Did you go to the movies last night? *A:* No, I went to Ginza. But I didn't see a movie. I had a meal. *B:* You did? You had a meal in Ginza? Ginza restaurants are expensive, aren't they. *A:* That's true. But I ate at a cheap restaurant. The meal was cheap. I didn't have beer. *B:* You didn't have beer? What did you drink? *A:* I drank tea. Beer is expensive.

Tea is cheap. *B:* Afterward, what did you do?
Did you run into (meet) anyone (you knew)? *A:*
No, I didn't run into anyone (I knew). I came home
early. I studied. *B:* What studying did you do?
Which studying did you do? Did you study your
English? *A:* No, I didn't study English. I studied
Japanese. It was my Japanese studying. I did
my Japanese studying. *B:* Did you study a lot?
How long was it? *A:* I studied for 4 hours. *B:*
Was your wife studying? Did your wife study,
last night? *A:* No, she wrote letters. After that
she read (a book).

Lesson 15
DO YOU? WILL YOU?

PHRASES

Do you do it? (*or* Will you do it?)	**Shimas' ka?**
every day (*or* all the time)	**mainichi**
Do you go (there) every day?	**Mainichi ikimas' ka?**
Are you going to-day?	**Kyō ikimas' ka?**
Will you go tomorrow?	**Ash'ta ikimas' ka?**
Won't you come this evening?	**Komban kimasen ka?**

61

together	issho-ni
Won't you eat with us?	Issho-ni tabemasen ka?
Won't you go with us? (or Please go with us.)	Issho-ni ikimasen ka?
Won't you sell that?	Sore urimasen ka?
I won't buy this.	Kore kaimasen.
Are you going home now?	Ima (or Mō) kaerimas'
Will you have beer?	Biiru nomimas' ka?
Don't you drink coffee? (or Won't you have some coffee?)	Kōhii nomimasen ka?
Will you see him tomorrow night?	Myōban kare ni aimas' ka?
Is this the way it's written?	Kō kakimas' ka?
You don't write it that way.	Sō kakimasen.
place	tokoro
How about (it)?	Dō des' ka? (or Ikaga des' ka?)
It's good. (or OK.)	Ii des'.
It's no good. (or No. or Don't!)	Dame des'.

PRACTICE

A: Komban gohan doko tabemas' ka, anta. Issho-ni tabemasen ka? B: Arigato. Dōmo. Nan-ji tabemas' ka? A: Sō des' ne. Roku-ji ii des' ka? B: Ii des'. Doko ikimas' ka? A: Sā, Ginza ikimasen ka? S'koshi takai des'. Sh'kashi, Ginza no gohan—ii des' ne. B: Sō des' ne. Sā, rokuji aimas' ne. A: Rokuji. Sayonara. B: Sayonara.

A: Komban wa. B: Komban wa. Ima ikimas' ka? A: Hai, kuruma des'. B: Anta, kuruma kaimash'ta ka? Itsu kaimash'ta? A: Iie, kaimasen desh'ta. Kore—ani ("big brother") no kuruma des' ne. Dōzo. B: Hai, dōmo. Ginza ikimas' ne. A: Sō des'. Hidari ikimas'. Sore kara migi ikimas'. Sore kara massugu des'. B: Ah, koko des' ne. Koko desh'ta ne. ("It was this place you meant, wasn't it?") A: Sō des'. Chotto matte ne. Ii des'. Koko des'.... Waitress: Komban wa. A: Komban wa. Waitress: Dōzo. A: Hai, dōmo. As'ko ii des' ka? Waitress: Hai, dōzo. Nani tabemas' ka? A: Sō des' ne. Karē-raisu ("rice-curry") arimas' ka? W: Arimas'. A: Ikaga des' ka, karē-raisu? B: Ii des'. Karē-raisu tabemas'. W: Futari, karē-raisu des' ka?

63

("The two of you—is it rice-curry?") Nani nomimas', ka? Biiru nomimas' ka? A: Biiru ippon ikaga des' ka, *Brown* san? B: Biiru dame des'. Miruku arimas' ka? W: Arimas'. Miruku nomimas' ka? B: Hai, miruku kudasai. A: Watashi—biiru ippon kudasai. W: Hai, hai. Chotto matte kudasai.... Dōzo.... A: Ii, des' ne, karē-raisu. Mō tabemash'ta ka? B: Hai, mō tabemash'ta. A: Chotto, nē-san ("waitress")! Chotto! W: Hai, hai. A: Ikura des' ka? W: Sō des' ne. Chotto matte kudasai. Karē-raisu futatsu—sam-byaku en, miruku hitotsu—nijū en, biiru ippon—hyaku ni-jū en. Minna—yon-hyaku yon-jū en des' ne. A: Hai, dōzo. W: Dōmo arigato gozaimash'ta. Mata dōzo. A: Sayonara.

B: Dōmo sumimasen desh'ta. Gochisō-sama (desh'ta) A: Dō itashimash'te. Soko no karē-raisu s'koshi takai des'. Sh'kashi ii des' ne, soko no gohan.

TIPS

Verbs in the polite present (" does do ") and definite future ("will do") end in -mas'; the negative (" does not do," "won't do ") ends in -masen. Notice that the object of the action precedes the verb, unlike English. Japanese verb expressions usually come at the end of a sentence, though you can always throw in other things as afterthoughts.

A: Where are you eating tonight? Shall we eat together? *B*: Thank you. Thanks. What time will we eat? *A*: Well let's see. Is 6 o'clock OK? *B*: It's OK. Where will we go? *A*: Well, why not go to the Ginza? It's a bit high. But Ginza meals are good, aren't they. Well, we'll meet at 6 then, right? *A*: At 6. Goodbye. *B*: Goodbye.

A: Good evening. *B*: Good evening. Are we going now? *A*: Yes, (it's by) car. *B*: Did you buy a car? When did you buy it? *A*: No, I didn't buy one. This is my (big) brother's car. Here, please (get in). *B*: Thank you. We're going to the Ginza, aren't we. *A*: That's right. We go left. Then we go right. Then it's straight ahead. *B*: Ah, here it is. It was this place (you meant), wasn't it? *A*: That's right. Wait just a minute. It's OK—this is the place.... *Waitress*: Good evening. *A*: Good evening. *Waitress*: Please (come this way). *A*: Thank you. Is it all right (to sit) over there? *Waitress*: Yes, please do. What will you have to eat? *A*: Let me see. Have you got rice-curry? *W*: Yes, we have. *A*: How about it, rice-curry? *B*: That's good. We'll eat rice-curry. *W*: Two rice-curries? What will you have to drink? Will you have beer? *A*: How about a bottle of beer, Mr. Brown? *B*: Beer's no good. (I'm off beer. I don't like beer. I don't want beer.) Have you got milk? *W*: Yes, we have. Will you have milk? *B*: Yes, milk please. *A*: Bring me a bottle of beer. *W*: Yes, sir. Just a moment.... Here, please (have your food).... *A*: It is good, isn't it, the rice-curry. Have you finished eating? *B*: Yes, I'm through (eating). *A*: Say, waitress! Waitress! *W*: Yes, sir. *A*: How much is it? (What's the bill?) *W*: Let's see now. Wait just a moment. 2 rice-curry—300 Yen, one milk—20 Yen, a bottle of beer—120 Yen. Altogether—it's 440 Yen. *A*: All right, here you are. *W*: Thank you very much. Come again. *A*: Goodbye.

B: Thank you very much. Thank you for the treat. *A*: Not at all. They charge a bit more for rice-curry there. But it's good, the meals you get there, isn't it.

Lesson 16

SHALL WE? LET'S!

PHRASES

Shall we go?	**Ikimashō ka?**
Yes, let's go.	**Hai, ikimashō.**
Let's go home now.	**Ima kaerimashō.**
Let's begin.	**Hajimemashō.**
Let's have a bottle of beer.	**Biiru ippon nomimashō.**
Let's have a smoke.	**Tabako nomimashō.**
Let's watch television.	**Terebi mimashō.**
Let's talk Japanese.	**Nihongo hanashimashō.**
Let's buy the tickets later.	**Kippu, ato de kaimashō.**
Shall we study?	**Benkyō shimashō ka?**
What might this be? (*or* What do	**Kore—nan deshō ka?**

you think this is?)	
It's probably medicine. (or I think it is medicine.)	Kusuri deshō ne.
Shall we have dinner together.	Ban-gohan issho-ni tabemashō ka?
I wonder whose it is.	Dare no deshō ka ne.
It must be Tanaka's.	Tanaka san no deshō ne.
I guess so.	Sō deshō.
Shall we (or I) go in?	Hairimashō ka?
Shall we (or I) go out?	Demashō ka?

PRACTICE

A: Komban issho-ni eiga mimashō ka?
B: Hai, mimashō. Doko no eigakan ikimashō ka? A: Sō des' ne. Doko ii deshō ka ne. B: Asak'sa ni eigakan tak'san arimas'. Asak'sa ikimashō. A: Sore ii deshō ne. Asak'sa no Kokusai Gekijō ("International Theater") no konshū no eiga—mimash'ta ka, anta? B: Mada des' ne. Sore mimashō ka? A: Hai, sō shimashō.

B: Ano eiga— ii des'. ne.   A: Hai,

67

ii eiga desh'ta. Ima nan-ji des' ka?
B: Mō ku-j des' ne. Sugu kaerimashō
ka? A: Ato de kaerimashō. Ima kōhii
nomimashō. Doko ii deshō ka? B: Kono
soba ni, Kōhi-ten arimas'. Ii tokoro des'.
A: Soko no kōhii—s'koshi takai deshō ne.
B: Iie, yasui des'. Yon-jū en des'. Hairi-
mashō.

Tips

Verb forms ending in -mashō are sugges-
tions; they mean "let's" or "shall we?"
but sometimes the meaning is "shall I?"
"let me," or "I think I'll." **Deshō**
means "it probably is," "I think it is,"
"it must be (I think)"; **deshō ka** means
"might it be?" "would it be?" "do you
think it is?" **Deshō ka ne** means "I wonder
if it is" or "I wonder if it probably is."
Sometimes **deshō** is used all by itself as an
afterthought sentence to mean "probably."

A: Shall we see a movie together tonight? *B*:
Yes, let's. What movie house shall we go to? *A*:
Let's see. Where would be good now? *B*: In
Asakusa there are lots of movies. Let's go to Asa-
kusa. *A*: That would be good, wouldn't it. Have
you seen this week's show at the International
Theater in Asakusa? *B*: Not yet. Shall we see
that? *A*: Yes, let's.

A: That movie was good, wasn't it. *A*: Yes,
it was a good film. What time is it now? *B*: It's
9 o'clock. Shall we go right home? *B*: Let's go
home later on. Let's have a cup of coffee now.

Where would be a good place? *B:* Nearby here there's a coffee-shop. It's a good place. *A:* The coffee there would be a bit expensive, wouldn't it? *B:* No, it's cheap. It's 40 Yen. Let's go in.

Lesson 17

WHAT KIND?

PHRASES

What kind of thing was it?	**Donna mono desh'ta ka?** (or **Dō-yū mono desh'ta ka?**)
Was it a big thing?	**Ōkii mono desh'ta ka?**
Was it a big one?	**Ōkii no desh'ta ka?**
Was it a little thing?	**Chiisai mono desh'ta ka?**
Was it a good thing?	**Ii mono desh'ta ka?**
Was it a bad (no-good) thing?	**Warui** (or **Dame na**) **mono desh'ta ka?**
Was it an interesting movie?	**Omoshiroi eiga desh'ta ka?**
Was it a dull story (*or* lecture)?	**Tsumaranai hanashi desh'ta ka?**
Was it a dull person?	**Tsumaranai hito desh'ta ka?**

69

Was it a young person?	Wakai hito desh'ta ka?
Was it Grandfather? (or Was it an old man?)	Ojii-san desh'ta ka?
Was it Uncle? or Was it a middle-aged man?	Oji-san desh'ta ka?
Was it Grandmother? (or Was it an old woman?)	Obā-san desh'ta ka?
Was it Aunt? (or Was it a middle-aged woman?)	Oba-san desh'ta ka?
white paper	shiroi kami
black shoes	kuroi kutsu
green socks	midori no kutsu-shita
a sick person	byōki no hito
a person in good spirits	genki na hito
Are you sick?	Byōki des' ka?
Are you in good health?	Genki des' ka?
a pretty girl	kirei na musume
a pretty room (or clean room)	kirei na heya
The girl is pretty.	Musume—kirei des'.
The room is clean (or pretty).	Heya—kirei des'.

70

I like this.	Kore s'ki des'.
This is something I like.	Kore—s'ki na mono des'.
I dislike this.	Kore—iya des'. (or kirai des')
This is something I dislike.	Kore—iya na (or kirai na) mono des'.

PRACTICE

A: Anta no uchi ōkii des' ne. Kirei des' ne. B: Dō itashimash'te. Chiisai tokoro des'. Kitanai ("dirty") tokoro des'. Gomen nasai ne. A: Kore—omoshiroi mono des' ne. Nan deshō ka? B: Sore—midori no za-buton ("seat-cushion") des'. Kanai kaimash'ta ne. Kanai—midori—s'ki des'. Anata—s'ki des' ka? A: Watashi—s'ki des', midori. Midori no mono—s'ki des'. Akai mono—chotto iya des' ne. Anata—donna mono s'ki des' ka? B: Sō des' ne. Watashi—kiiroi ("yellow") mono s'ki des' ne. Sore—chiisai mono des' ne. Ōkii mono—kuroi mono s'ki des'. Kuroi kuruma s'ki des'. A: Sō des' ka. Watashi no kuruma—kuroi des'.

A: Sakuban kirei na musume ni aimash'ta. B: Sō des' ka? Sore—omoshiroi des' ne. Doko desh'ta ka? A: Tomodachi no uchi desh'ta. Sono tomo-

71

**dachi no imōto des'. Sono namae ("her
name")—Fumiko des'.   B: Omoshiroi
deshō ne, sore. Ato de. mata ("again")
aimas' ka? A: Hai, mata aimas'. Raishū deshō ne. B: Watashi—kirei na musume, s'ki des'. Issho-ni sono musume ni
aimashō ka?   Iie, iie. Sumimasen ga
("but") ne, hitori—ii des', futari—dame
des'. B: Shitsurei desh'ta. Gomen nasai.**

TIPS

English adjectives correspond to 3 different kinds of words in Japanese. One kind,
Japanese adjectives, can be used right in
front of a noun like English adjectives: **ōkii
des'** "is big" and **ōkii uchi** "big house,"
kuroi des' "is black" and **kuroi kutsu**
"black shoes." Others, Japanese nouns
(despite their meaning), need the word **no**
to link them with the following noun: **midori des'** "is green"; but **midori no zabuton ;** "a green seat-cushion" **byōki des'**
"is sick" but **byōki no hito** "a sick person." The third kind use the word **na** to
link with a noun: **genki des'** "is in good
health" but **genki na hito** "a person in
good health" **kirei des'** "is pretty (or
clean)" but **kirei na musume** "a pretty
girl." We call the third kind copular nouns,
but you may find it simpler to think of them
as "na-words."

72

A: Your house is big, isn't it. It's nice (pretty).
B: Not at all. It's a small place. It's a dirty place.
Excuse me (for its being in such a mess). *A*: This
is an interesting thing. What could it be? *B*:
That's a green seat-cushion. My wife bought it.
My wife likes green. Do you like it? *A*: Yes, I
like it, green. Green things I like. Red things I'm
not too fond of. What sort of thing do you like?
B: Well, let's see. I like yellow things, you know.
That (is)—(if) it's a little thing. (If it is) a big
thing—I like black things. I like black cars. *A*:
Oh? My car is black.

A: Last night I met a pretty girl. *B*: You did?
That's interesting. Where was it? *A*: It was at
a friend's house. She's the younger sister of my
friend. Her name is Fumiko. *B*: That must have
been fun. Will you see her again sometime (in the
future)? *A*: Yes, I'll see her again. It'll be next
week. *B*: I like pretty girls. Shall we see that
girl together? *A*: No, no. I'm sorry, but, you
know, one is fine, but two—it's no good. *B*: I've
been rude. Excuse me.

Lesson 18

IS, AM, AND ARE

Phrases

There is. (*or* We have got some.)	**Arimas'.**
There is some there. (*or* It is there. *or* We've	**Soko ni arimas'.**

got some there.)

Somebody stays (there). (*or* Somebody is around. Somebody is alive. *or* There is somebody (there.)	**imas'.**
Who is here?	**Dare koko ni imas' ka?**
What is here?	**Nani koko ni arimas' ka?**
Is there anyone there? (*or* Are people present? (*or* Are people staying?)	**Hito imas' ka?**
Do we have any people? (*or* Are there people?)	**Hito arimas' ka?**
Do you have an older brother?	**Nii-san arimas' ka?**
Is your brother around? (*or* Is your brother alive?)	**Nii-san imas' ka?**
Where are you now?	**Anata ima doko ni imas' ka?**
Is it you (I am	**Anata des' ka?**

74

talking to)?

Where is it (that you are at)? **Doko des' ka?**

PRACTICE

Tanaka: **Moshi moshi.** Nakamura: **Moshi moshi.** T: **Sumimasen. Nakamura san des' ka?** N: **Sō des'. Dare des' ka?** T: **Koko—Tanaka des'. Watashi—Tanaka.** N: **Ah, sō des' ka. Ano ne, Tanaka san.** T: **Ha.** ("yes," a brief way to say hai on the telephone) N: **Anta no uchi ikimash'ta ga ne** ("but...") T: **Ha.** N: **Rokuji desh'-ta ga ne...** T: **Ha.** N: **Anta imasen desh'ta ne.** T: **Ha, Sō des'.** **Imasen desh'ta. Dōmo sumimasen desh'ta.** N: **Ima uchi des' ka? Ima uchi ni imas' ka?** T: **Iie, chigaimas'.** (" It's not like that—it's different.") N: **Doko ni imas' ka?** T: **Ima ne...** N: **Ha.** T: **Uchi ni imasen ne, watashi.** N: **Ha.** T: **Ani no tokoro** ("my brother's") **ni imas'.** N: **Ah, sō des' ka? Nii-san no uchi des' ka?** T: **Hai, sore kara ne** ("and then...") N: **Ha.** T: **Nii-san no hanashi desu ga ne...** ("it is but...") N: **Ha.** T: **Komban ii eiga arimas' ne.** N: **Sō des' ka? Sore—doko des' ka? Sono eiga doko ni arimas' ka?** T: **Ani no uchi no sugu soba** ("right next ro ") des' Soba no eigakan des'. N: Sō des' ka? Sono eiga ikimas' ka? T: Ikimas'. Issho ni ikimasen ka? N: Sō des' ne. Nan-ji deshō ka, sono eiga. T: Hachi-ji han des'. Daijōbu des'. ("It's OK [—you've got plenty of time].") Ikimashō. Sono eiga mimashō. N: Hai. Ikimas'. Matte kudasai ne. T: Hai, daijōbu des'. Hayaku ne. Sayonara. N: Sayonara. Shitsurei shimash'ta.

TIPS

Notice the difference in meaning between **arimas'** "there is," "something or someone exists," "we have something or someone," **imas'** "he is," "someone is alive, is in a place, or stays in a place," and . . .**des'** "it is (something)," "it equals (something)." In some cases, you could get by with any of the three, with only a slight difference of meaning. But often you will have to pick just one of the three to translate your English "is." Choose **arimas'** if you can replace the "is" with "we've got" and still make some sense; with **imas'** if you can replace "is" with "lives" or "stays"; with **des'** if you can replace "is" with "equals" or "is the same as." And notice that the English word "is" sometimes has the shapes "am," "are," "be"; the past (**arimash'ta, imash'ta,** or **desh'ta**) has the shapes "was" and "were" in English.

Tanaka: Hello. *Nakamura*: Hello. *T:* Excuse me. Is this Mr. Nakamura? *N*: Yes, it is. Who is it? *Tanaka*: Here (at this end)—it's Tanaka. I'm Tanaka. *N*: Oh. Say Mr. Tanaka. *T*: Yes. *N*: I went to your house, but you know... *T*: Uh-huh. *N*: It was 6 o'clock but... *T*: Uh-huh. *N*: You weren't there. *T*: Yeah, that's right. I wasn't there. I'm very sorry. *N*: Are you at home now? *T*: No, I'm not. *N*: Where are you? *T*: Right now, you see... *N*: Uh-huh. *T*: I'm not at home, you see... *N*: Uh-huh. *T*: I'm at my (older) brother's. *N*: Oh, are you? It's your brother's house (you're at)? *T*: Yes, and then, you see... *N*: Yeah. *T*: It is what my brother was saying but... *N*: Uh-huh. *T*: There's a good movie on tonight. *N*: There is? Where is it? Where is the movie? *T*: It's right next to my brother's house. It's the movie house right nearby. *N*: It is? Are you going to that movie? *T*: We are. Why don't we go together? *N*: Well, let me think. What time would it be, that movie? *T*: It's 8:30. You've plenty of time. Let's go. Let's take in that movie. *N*: OK. I'm coming. Wait, won't you. *T*: Yes, don't worry. Come quick, though. Goodbye. *N*: Goodbye. I've been rude.

Lesson 19

WHAT'S DOING?

Phrases

What are you do-ing?	**Nani sh'te imas' ka?**
I'm talking Japanese.	**Nihongo hanash'te imas'.**

What were you doing last night?	Yūbe nani sh'te imash'ta ka?
I was watching television.	Terebi mite imash'ta.
My wife was writing letters.	Kanai tegami kaite imash'ta.
Where do they sell cars? (*or* Where is there a car dealer?)	Kuruma doko utte imas' ka?
Where will you sell your car?	Kuruma doko urimas' ka?
What are you saying?	Nani itte (*or* yutte) imas' ka?
Where did the child go to? (*or* Where is the child?)	Kodomo doko itte imas' ka?
Has your friend arrived? (*or* Is your friend here?)	Tomodachi kite imas' ka?
Did your friend come?	Tomodachi kimash'ta ka?
Did you get tired?	Ts'karemash'ta ka?
Are you tired?	Ts'karete imas' ka?
Did you understand? (*or* Was it clear?)	Wakarimash'ta ka?
Is it understood? (*or* Is everything	Wakatte imas' ka?

78

.. clear?)

How long did you rest (or sleep)?	Nan-jikan yasumima-sh'ta ka?
Is the child resting (or sleeping) now?	Kodomo ima yasunde imas' ka?
Are you drinking beer?	Biiru nonde imas' ka?
Will you have some beer? (or Do you drink beer?)	Biiru nomimas' ka?
Are you listening to the radio?	Rajio kiite imas' ka?
At that time I was eating, you see.	Sono toki gohan tabe-te imash'ta ne.

PRACTICE

A: Kinō nani sh'te imash'ta ka? B: Watashi des' ka? Kinō des' ka? Sō des' ne. Sā, asa — benkyō sh'te imash'ta ne, yo-jikan. Hiru kara, shigoto sh'te imash'ta. Anta—dō desh'ta ka? ("How was it?"="What were you up to?") A: Yasunde imash'ta. Uchi des'ne. Terebi mite imash'ta. Omoshiroi desh'ta. Hito ni shitsumon ("questions") kiite imash'ta ne. ("They were asking people questions.") Sore kara, o-kane kurete imash'ta ("they

79

were giving"). B: **O-kane tak'san kuremash'ta ka?** A: **Hai. Hitori no onna ni ne,
jū-man en kuremash'ta.** B: **Sō des' ka?
Ii des' ne—sore. Komban uchi ni imas'
ka, anta?** A: **Hai, imas'. Kimasen ka?
Watashi komban terebi mite imas'. Issho
ni mimashō.** B: **Dōmo arigato gozaimas'.**

A: **Sakuban rajio o kiite imash'ta ka?**
B: **Iie, kiite imasen desh'ta. Eiga mite
imash'ta.** A: **Sō des' ka. Sakuban no
rajio- omoshiroi hanashi desh'ta.** B:
Dare hanashimash'ta ka? A: **Amerika-
jin hitori hanash'te imash'ta.** B: **Nani
itte imash'ta ka?** A: **Tada-ima** ("just
now") **Nihon ni kimash'ta, kono Amerika-
jin ne.** B: **Nihon s'ki desh'ta ka, sono
hito?** A: **Hai, sō itte imash'ta. Nihon
s'ki des'.**

A: **Gomen kudasai!** B: **Hai, hai. Dare
des' ka?** A: **Sumimasen ga, danna-san
imas' ka?** B: **Imasen. Gakkō ni
ikimash'ta. Sugu kaerimas'. Matte kudasai ne.** A: **Dōmo...** C: **Tadaima!** ("I'm
back just now"—said on returning to your
residence) **Tadaima kaerimash'ta!** B: **Oka-
eri nasai!** ("Please come home"—said to
a person returning to his residence). **Oka-
eri nasai, danna san. Dōzo.** C: **Hai, dō-**

mo. B: Ano ne, danna-san. C: Hai. B:
O-kyaku san ("guest") kite imas'. A: Sō
des' ka? O-kyaku des' ka? Doko ni
imas' ka? B: As'ko ni matte imas'. C:
Gomen nasai. Dōmo shitsurei shimash'ta.
Anata—matte imash'ta. Sore—dōmo sumimasen desh'ta. A: Iie, iie. Dō itashimash'te. Watashi hayaku kimash'ta. Shitsurei shimash'ta.

TIPS

The construction **-te imas'** consists of the
gerund or **-te** form of a verb + the verb **imas'**
The most common meaning is "is doing
something" or "will be doing something"
—emphasizing the duration of an action:
matte imas' "I am waiting" or "I will be
waiting." The **-te** form corresponds to the
English "-ing," and the verb **imas'** corresponds to the English "is." But there are some
Japanese verbs which refer to actions thought
of as incapable of duration (**ts'karemas'**
"gets tired," **wakarimas'** "catches on," or
"gets understood," **ikimas'** "goes," **kimas'**
"comes"). With these verbs, the construction **-te imas'** means "is in a state resulting
from the action," so **ts'karete imas'** means
"is tired," **wakatte imas'** means "is understood," "is known," **itte imas'** means "is
(gone) there," **kite imas'** means "is come,"
"is (arrived) here." There are a few other

81

Japanese verbs which take the **-te imas'** form just to show habitual action (**kuruma utte imas'** "they sell cars") in order to distinguish from the present-future form (**kuruma urimas'** "they will sell the car"). The shapes of the gerund forms are a bit complicated to explain; sometimes they end in **-te** sometimes in **-de.** You will find it easiest just to learn the gerund for each verb separately: **urimas'** "buys," **utte** "buying." Notice that **itte** is the gerund for both **iimas'** "says" and **ikimas'** "goes," so **itte imas'** can mean either "is saying" or "is (gone) there," but downtown Tokyo people say **yutte imas'** for "is saying."

A: What were you doing yesterday? *B*: Me? Yesterday? Let's see. Why, in the morning I was studying you know, 4 hours. In the afternoon, I was working. What were you up to? *A*: I was loafing (resting). I was at home. I was watching television. It was amusing. They were asking people questions, you see. And then, they were giving them money. *B*: Did they give away lots of money? *A*: They gave one woman 10,000 Yen *B*: They did? That's nice. Are you going to be at home tonight? *A*: Yes, I will be. Won't you come? I'm going to be watching television. Let's watch it together. *B*: Thank you very much.

A: Were you listening to the radio last night? *B*: No, I wasn't. I was seeing a movie. *A*: Oh? It was interesting, what they were saying (the talk) on the radio last night. *B*: Who talked? *A*: There was an American talking. *B*: What was he saying? *A*: He's just arrived in Japan, this American, see. *B*: Did he like Japan, that man. *A*: Yes, that's what he was saying. He likes Japan.

A : Excuse me (anybody home)! B : Yes sir. Who is it? A : Excuse me, is the gentleman of the house at home? B : He's already gone out. He went to the school. He'll be right back. Won't you wait? A : Thank you.... C : Hello—I'm back. I've come back home. B : Welcome home. Welcome home, master (or husband). Here (come in, put on these slippers, etc.). C : Ah, thank you. B : By the way, master (or husband). C : Yes? B : There's a guest here. A : There is? There's a guest? Where is he? B : He's waiting in there. C : Excuse me. I've been very rude. You were waiting. I'm very sorry about that. A : No, no. Not at all. I came early. I was rude.

Lesson 20

PLEASE DO!

PHRASES

Please give me some coffee.	Kōhii kudasai.
I'd like some coffee please.	Kōhii negaimas'.
Please. (or Please ! or Please do !— said either to gain attention in a shop or after making a request)	Negaimas'.

Please drink some coffee.	Kōhii nonde kudasai.
Please come this evening.	Komban kite kudasai.
Go fast. (or Talk fast.)	Hayaku itte kudasai.
Say it once more please.	Mō ichido itte kudasai.
Take a look at this.	Kore mite kudasai.
Please talk slow.	Yukkuri hanash'te kudasai.
Ask the policeman.	Omawari-san ni kiite kudasai.
Eat a little more, please.	Mō s'koshi tabete kudasai.
Please write me a letter.	Watashi ni tegami kaite kudasai.
Please mail the letter.	Tegami dash'te kudasai.
Please call me on the phone.	Denwa kakete kudasai.
Is it the phone? (or Is it a phone call?)	Denwa des' ka?
Did you phone me?	Watashi ni denwa kakemash'ta ka?
Did you write a letter?	Tegami kakimash'ta ka?

Did you wire (send a telegram)?   Dempō uchimash'ta ka?

Please wire.   Dempō utte kudasai.

Is it a telegram?   Dempō des' ka?

You'll phone, won't you?   Denwa kakete ne!

Take care of yourself now! So long!   Ki o ts'kete ne!

PRACTICE

N: Tanaka san, Tanaka san! Chotto matte kudasai. T: Nakamura san des' ka? Konnichi wa. N: Konnichi wa. Ima doko ikimas' ka? T: Ima sampo ("a walk") sh'te imas'. Issho ni sampo sh'te kudasai. N: Ha, arigato gozaimas'. S'koshi sampo shimashō. Ano ne. Are mite kudasai. Nan deshō ka? T: Sō des' ne. Hito tak'san imas' ne. Nani sh'te imas' ka ne. N: Hito tak'san kite imas' ne. Ah, wakarimash'ta! Demo ("political demonstration," "rally") des' ne. T: Sō deshō ne. Demo deshō. N: Anta ts'karete imas' ka? T: Hai, s'koshi ts'karemash'ta. ("I've gotten a little tired.") N: Yasunde kudasai. Koko—yasumimashō. Demo mimashō.

N: Tanaka san, komban watashi no

85

uchi ni ne, kite kudasai. Uchi no ("our,"
"the one at our house") terebi mite kudasai.
T: Arigato gozaimas'. Nan-ji ni kimashō
ka. (Here kimashō means "shall I come?")
N: Sā, roku-ji ni kite kudasai ne. Issho ni
ban-gohan tabete ne. Sore kara terebi
mite ne. T: Ha, dōmo. Anta no tokoro
—watashi yoku wakarimasen ne. Hakkiri
itte kudasai ("Tell me clearly—how to get
there"). N: Sō des' ne. Eki demas' ne.
Sore kara migi itte ne. Gakkō arimas'.
Gakkō no soba, hidari itte ne. Sore kara
ōkii pachinko-ya ("pinball parlor") des' ne.
Pachinko-ya no soba ni, kōban ("police
box") arimas'. Kōban no omawari-san
ni kiite kudasai ne. Sugu soba des'. Wakarimash'ta ka? T: Ha, wakarimash'ta.
Dōmo. Sayonara. N: Sayonara. Ki o
ts'kete ne!

TIPS

Kudasai by itself means "please give."
The expression -te kudasai means "please
do something." You have already encoun-
tered it in the expression Chotto matte kudasai "Please wait a minute." You can
add the particle ne: Chotto matte kudasai
ne. Or you can drop the kudasai and just
use gerund + ne: Chotto matte ne. This
is a very familiar, friendly way to ask some-

one to do something. You find this form in
the common expression **Ki o ts'kete ne!**
"Take care of yourself! So long!"

N: Mr. Tanaka, Mr. Tanaka! Wait a minute!
T: Is it Mr. Nakamura? Hello. *N*: Hello. Where
are you going now? *T*: I'm taking a walk. Take
a walk with me. *N*: Thank you. Let's take a
little walk. Say. Look at that over there. I wonder
what it is. *T*: Yes, now, let's see. There are lots
of people there. I wonder what they're doing. *N*:
Lots of people have arrived, haven't they. Ah, I've
got it (understood it)! It's a political demonstration (rally) isn't it. *T*: I guess it is, isn't it. It
must be a demonstation. *N*: Are you tired? *T*:
Yes, I've gotten a little tired. *N*: Rest a bit. Let's
rest here. Let's watch the demonstration.

N: Mr. Tanaka, come to my house tonight, won't
you. Watch our television. *T*: Thank you. What
time shall I come? *N*: Why, come at 6. We'll eat
together. Then we'll watch television. *T*: Fine,
thank you. Your place—I don't understand very
well (how to get there). *N*: Well let's see. You go
out of the station. Then go right. There's a
school. Near the school go left. Then there is
a large pinball parlor. Next to the pinball parlor
there is a police-box. Ask the policeman in the
police-box. It's right nearby. Have you got it?
T: Yes, I understand. Thank you. Goodbye. *N*:
Goodbye. Take it easy.

PART III

Sprinkle in a Few Particles

Lesson 21

WHERE FROM? WHERE TO?

PHRASES

where from?	doko kara?
where to?	doko e? or doko made?
from here to there	koko kara as'ko made (or koko kara as'ko e)
has (*or* has got *or* is holding)	motte imas'
is holding in one's hand	te ni motte imas'
brings	motte kimas'
takes	motte ikimas'
I give it to you.	Watashi anata ni agemas'.
You give it to him.	Anata kare ni agemas'.
Tanaka gives it to him.	Tanaka san kare ni agemas'.
He gives it to you.	Kare anata ni kuremas'.
He gives it to me.	Kare watashi ni kuremas'.

You give it to me.	**Anta watashi ni kuremas'.**
Who did you get it from?	**Dare kara moraimash'ta ka?**
Who got (received) it?	**Dare moraimash'ta ka?**
Will you get (receive) it?	**Moraimas' ka?**

PRACTICE

A: **Nani motte kimash'ta ka, anta? Nani motte imas' ka, te ni? Te ni nani motte imas' ka?** B: **Watashi des' ka? Kore des' ka? Ah, kore ne—dempō des'. Watashi dempō moraimash'ta.** A: **Dare kara moraimash'ta ka, sono dempō?** B: **Tanaka san kara des'. Tanaka san ash'ta koko e kimas'. Tōkyō e kimas' ne.** A: **Doko kara kimas' ka?** B: **Ōsaka kara kimas'. Ima Ōsaka ni imas' ne. Sengetsu soko e ikimash'ta. Ash'ta watashi ni, Ōsaka kara no mono motte kimas'.** A: **Sō des' ka? Shigoto no mono des' ka?** B: **Sō des'. Ōsaka no kōba ("factory") kara no mono des' ne. Tanaka san, sono mono, watashi ni kuremas'. Dempō mite kudasai ne.** A: **Watashi. Nihongo no dempō, wakarimasen ne. Sumimasen. Ano ne. Ōsaka kara, Tōkyō made, nan-**

jikan kakarimas' ka. B: Sō des' ne.
Hachi-jikan deshō ne, Osaka kara Tōkyō
made. Sā, uchi ni denwa kakemashō
ne. ("I think I'll just phone home..." *or*
"Let me just phone home...") Chotto.
Mā! o-kane arimasen ne. Jū en kurema-
sen ka? A: Agemas'. Koko ni arimas',
jū en. Dōzo. B: Hai, dōmo.

B: Moshi moshi. Maid: Moshi moshi.
B: Ano ne. Ok'-san imas'ka? M: Imasen,
ok'-san. B: Sō des' ka? Ok'-san ni itte
kudasai ne. M: Ha. B: Dempō morai-
mash'ta ne. M: Ha. B: Sono dempō no
hanashi des' ne. M: Ha. B: Tanaka san
kara no dempō des' ne. M: Ha. B:
Tanaka san kimas' ne. Ashita kimas' ne.
M: Ha. Ha. B: Ok'-san ni ne. M: Ha.
B: Sō itte kudasai ne. M: Hai. Iimas'.
Ok'-san ni iimas' ne. B: Dōmo. Shitsurei.
Sayonara. M: Sayonara. Dōmo. Shitsurei.

A: Ok'-san imash'ta ka? B: Iie, jochū
desh'ta. Jochū ni iimash'ta. Jochū—
kanai ni iimas' ne, ato de. A: Dempō
jimusho e motte ikimas' ka? B: Hai
motte ikimas'. Jimusho no hito ni misemas' ("will show"). Issho ni kimas' ka?
A:Iie, sumimasen. Yōji ("some business")
arimas'. Ato de aimashō. Komban aima-

shō ne. B: Ii des'. Mata Konban ne. Sayonara. Shitsurei shimash'ta. B: Sayonara. Shitsurei shimas'.

Tips

Particles are little words Japanese tack on to show more exactly what the preceding words are doing in the sentence. In some cases, they correspond to English prepositions, except that they come after the noun, rather than before: **koko kara** "from here," **soko made** "to there," **Tōkyō e** "to Tokyo," **anta ni** "to you," **anta no tokoro e** "to your place." Notice that **kara** sometimes means "after" as well as "from": **ash'ta kara** "from tomorrow" or "after tomorrow," **sore kara** "after that." For " to " you have had three particles —**e**, **made**, and **ni**. Ni has a terribly general meaning, so when it is a question of real physical direction in space, it is better to use **e** or **made**. These two are very similar in meaning, and you can use them more or less interchangeably ; the difference is that **e** focuses your attention on the goal (destination), and **made** calls attention to the trip between (in terms of time, distance, pleasantness, etc.), Sometimes **made** is translated "up to" or "as far as." There are two different words for " give " depending on just who gives whom: **agemas'** (sometimes **yarimas'**) means someone in the IN-GROUP gives to someone in the OUT-GROUP; **kure-mas'** (sometimes **kudasaimas'**) means someone in the OUT-GROUP gives to someone in the IN-GROUP. The in-group always includes "ME," the out-group usually includes "HIM." "YOU" are in the out-group with respect to "ME," but in the in-group with respect to "HIM."

A: What have you brought? What do you have there in your hand? What are you holding? *B*: Me? This? Oh, this thing, you mean—it's a telegram. I got a telegram. *A*: Who did you get it from, that telegram? *B*: It's from Mr. Tanaka. Mr. Tanaka is coming here tomorrow. He's coming to Tokyo, you see. *A*: Where is he coming from? *B*: He is coming from Osaka. He's in Osaka now, you know. He went there last month. Tomorrow he's bringing me some things from Osaka. *A*: Are they things connected with your job? *B*: That's right. They are things from the Osaka factory. Mr. Tanaka is giving me those things. Take a look at the telegram. (*or* Read the telegram.) *A*: I don't understand telegrams in Japanese. I'm sorry. Uh... how long does it take from Osaka to Tokyo? *B*: Let's see. It must be 8 hours, from Osaka to Tokyo. Well, I think I'll give my wife a call (and tell her about it). Excuse me a moment. Well, what do you know, I haven't got any money. Won't you give me 10 Yen. *A*: Sure (I'll give it to you). Here it is, 10 Yen. Here (please take it). *B*: Ah, thank you.

B: Hello. *M*: Hello. *B*: Uh... is Mrs. B. at home? *M*: She's not in, Mrs. B. *B*: Oh? Look, tell her for me, huh? *M*: Uh-huh. *B*: I got a telegram, see. *M*: Uh-huh. *B*: It's about that telegram, see. *M*: Uh-huh. *B*: It's a telegram from Mr. Tanaka, see. *M*: Uh-huh. *B*: Mr. Tanaka is coming, see. He's coming tomorrow, see. *M*:

Mm, uh-huh. *B*: (Now when you see) Mrs. B., see... *M*: Uh-huh. *B*: Tell her that, see. *M*: Yes. I'll tell her. I'll tell Mrs. B. *B*: Thank you. (I'm being) rude. Goodbye. *M*: Goodbye. Excuse me. (I'm being) rude. Goodbye.

A: Was your wife in? *B*: No, it was the maid. I told the maid. The maid will tell my wife, you see—later on. *A*: Are you going to take the telegram to your office? *B*: I'll take it. I'll show it to the people at the office. Will you come along? *A*: No, I'm sorry, but I've got some business. See you later. See you this evening, right? *B*: OK. Till this evening then. Goodbye. I've been rude. *A*: Goodbye. I've been rude.

Lesson 22

WHERE SHALL WE EAT?

PHRASES

Where shall we eat?	Doko de tabemashō ka?
Let's eat at a *sushi* shop.	Sushi-ya de tabemashō.
Do you like *sushi* (pickled-rice)?	O-sushi s'ki des' ka?
Fried shrimp. Chinese noodles. A noodlestand.	Tempura. O-soba. Soba-ya.
Where is the *sushi* maker?	Sushi-ya san doko ni imas' ka?

Where does he work?	Doko de shigoto shi-mas' ka?
Where are you working?	Anata doko de shigoto sh'te imas' ka?
Where are you?	Anata doko ni imas' ka?
Where's the saké?	O-sake doko ni arimas' ka?
Where do they make saké?	O-sake doko de ts'kurimas' ka?
What do they make saké out of?	O-sake nan de ts'kurimas' ka?
They make it out of raw rice.	O-kome de ts'kurimas' ne.
Where do they grow rice?	Kome doko de ts'kurimas' ka?
Where is it produced?	Doko de dekimas' ka?
Did you come by train?	Kisha de kimash'ta ka?
Is the train ready? (or Were you able to make it by train?)	Kisha dekimash'ta ka?
Did you come by electric train (or streetcar)?	Densha de kimash'ta ka?
Are you going by boat?	Fune de ikimas' ka?

Are you going by Hikōki de ikimas' ka?
plane?

PRACTICE

A: Komban doko de tabemashō ka?
B: Sō des' ne. Anata—o-sushi s'ki des' ka?
A: O-sushi s'koshi iya des' ne. Tempura
s'ki des'. B: Tempura s'ki des' ka?
Ginza ni ii tokoro arimas'. Soko e iki-
mashōka? Soko de tabemashō ka? A:
Sō des' ne. Soko de—tempura takai deshō ne. B: Iie, iie. Soko no tempura
yasui des'. Soko e ikimashō. Soko de
tabemashō. A: Nan de ikimas' ka, Ginza
made? Densha des' ka? Bas' ("bus")
des' ka? B: Iie. Koko kara ne—chikatetsu ("subway") arimas'. Chikatetsu de
ikimas'. Chikatetsu de ikimashō, Ginza
made.

A: Anata doko kara kimash'ta ka? B:
Amerika kara kimash'ta. A: Itsu kimash'ta ka? B: Kyonen kimash'ta ne, Nihon e. A: Amerika kara Nihon made,
nan de kimash'ta ka? B: Fune desh'ta.
Fune de kimash'ta. Ni-shūkan kakari-
mash'ta. A: Itsu kaerimas' ka, Amerika
e? B: Raigetsu des' ne. Raigetsu kaerimas'. A: Fune de kaerimas' ka? B: Iie,
hikōki de kaerimas'. A: Amerika ni ok'-

san arimas' ka ? ("Do you have a wife in America?") B: **Arimas'. Kanai —watashi matte imas' ne, Amerika de. Watashi— Nihon de shigoto sh'te imasu ga** ("am working, but"), **kanai —Amerika de matte imas' ne.**

TIPS

For the meaning "at," "in," etc. you use the particle **ni** only with verbs showing location—mostly **arimas'** and **imas'**. In other cases you use the particle **de** which means something like " HAPPENS at," "HAPPENS in," etc. For a very few cases, either particle is all right ; "Where are you living?" is either **Doko ni sunde imas' ka ?** or **Doko de sunde imas' ka ?** Notice that adjective expressions usually occur with no particle (or **de**): **Amerika ii des' ne.** "It's nice in America, isn't it?" **Koko kirei des' ne.** "It's pretty here." Two other meanings of the particle **de** are to show material (" What is it made of ?" **Nan de ts'kurimas' ka ?** or **Nan de dekite imas' ka ?**) and to show means (" I came by car." **Kuruma de kimash'ta.** " I am writing with a ball-point pen." **Bōru-pen de kaite imas'.** " I eat with chopsticks." **O-hashi de tabemas'.**) Still another meaning is found in **Nihongo de hanash'te kudasai.** "Please talk in Japanese." Notice the different words for rice: **kome** (or **o-kome**) is what grows in the field, or what you buy at the store, and **gohan** (or **meshi**) is what you eat (cooked rice). When served on a plate, American-style, instead of in a bowl, Japanese call it **rais'**

A: Tonight where shall we eat? *B*: Let's see. Do you like *sushi*? *A*: I'm not too fond of *sushi*, you know. I like *tempura*. *B*: You like *tempura*? There's a good place in Ginza. Shall we go there? Shall we eat there? *A*: Let's see. The *tempura* would be expensive there, wouldn't it? *B*: No, not at all. The *tempura* there is cheap. Let's go there. Let's eat there. *A*: What shall we go on, to Ginza? Streetcar? Bus? *B*: No. From here—there is a subway. We'll go by subway. Let's go by subway, as far as Ginza.

A: Where did you come from? *B*: I came from America. *A*: When did you come? *B*: I came last year, to Japan. *A*: What did you come on, from America to Japan? *B*: It was a boat. I came on a boat. It took two weeks. *A*: When are you going home, to America. *B*: It's next month. I'm going home next month. *A*: Are you going back by boat? *B*: No, I'm going back by plane. *A*: Do you have a wife in America? *B*: Yes, I have. My wife is waiting for me, in America. I am working in Japan, but my wife is waiting in America.

Lesson 23

ME TOO; ME NEITHER

Phrases

This is a newspaper.	Kore shimbun des'.
That is a newspaper too?	Sore mo shimbun des'.
I am reading.	Watashi yonde imas'.
Are you reading too?	Anta mo yonde imas' ka?
You are not eating.	Anta tabete imasen.
I am not eating either.	Watashi mo tabete imasen.
Do you eat meat?	Niku tabemas' ka?
Do you eat fish too?	Sakana mo tabemas' ka?
Do you eat both meat and fish?	Niku mo sakana mo tabemas' ka?
I eat neither meat nor fish. (or I don't eat either meat or fish.)	Niku mo sakana mo tabemasen.
Don't you eat either meat or fish?	Niku mo sakana mo tabemasen ka?

101

Practice

A: Watashi—byōki des'. B: Watashi
mo s'koshi byōki des' ne. Sakuban sakana
tabemash'ta ne, watashi. Anta mo sakana tabemash'ta ka? B: Hai, watashi mo
sakana tabemash'ta. Sono sakana dame
("bad") desh'ta ka ne. B: Sō deshō ne.
Watashi mo, anta mo, futari mo ("the
both of us") warui sakana tabemash'ta.
Da kara ne ("and so")—byōki des'. A:
Watashi kusuri nomimashō. Anta mo
kusuri nomimas' ka? B: Nomimasen.
Dōmo. Mō tak'san nomimash'ta, kusuri
ne. Kusuri mo, mizu mo, tak'san nomimash'ta. Da kara, mō nomimasen ne.

Tips

The particle **mo** means "also," "too"; but
if the sentence is negative, the English translation is "neither" or "either." Reference
is to the immediately preceding word; in
this respect Japanese is less ambiguous than
English. "I ate fish too." can mean two
different things: **Watashi mo sakana tabemash'ta.** "In addition to you, I also ate
fish." and **Watashi sakana mo tabemash'ta.**
"In addition to other food, I also ate fish."
In Japanese you have to decide just which
word the "too" refers to. When you have
two nouns each followed by **mo**, the English
translation is "either... or..."; for a nega-

tive sentence "neither... nor...." **Pan mo, yasai mo, arimas'.** "We've got both bread and vegetables." **Pan mo, yasai mo, arimasen.** "We don't have either bread or vegetables," or "we have neither bread nor vegetables." Sometimes **mo** follows another particle: **Tōkyō kara mo, Ōsaka kara mo, tegami kimash'ta.** "Letters came both from Tokyo and from Osaka." **Yokohama e mo ikimas' ka?** "Are you going to Yokohama too?" **Yokohama e mo ikimasen ka?** "Aren't you going to Yokohama either?"

A: I'm sick. *B*: I'm not feeling so well either. I ate fish last night. Did you eat fish too? *A*: Yes, I ate fish too. I wonder if that fish was bad? *B*: I bet it was. Both you and me, the two of us, we ate bad fish. And so—we're sick. *A*: I think I'll take some medicine. Will you have some medicine? *B*: No. Thank you. I've already taken a lot—of medicine. Both medicine and water I've drunk a lot. So, now I won't take any (more).

Lesson 24
WHO DOES WHAT?

PHRASES

Who does what?	**Dare ga nani o shimas' ka?**
Who is looking?	**Dare ga mite imas' ka?**

I am looking.	**Watashi ga mite imas'.**
Who are you looking at?	**Dare o mite imas' ka?**
I am looking at you.	**Anta o mite imas'.**
Who studies?	**Dare ga benkyō shimas' ka?**
Who studies this?	**Dare ga kore o benkyō shimas' ka?**
Who studies Japanese?	**Dare ga Nihongo o benkyō shimas' ka?** (or **Dare ga Nihongo no benkyō o shimas' ka?**)

PRACTICE

A: **Dare ga tabete imas' ka? Dare ga gohan tabete imas' ka? Dare ga gohan o tabete imas' ka?** B: **Watashi des'. Watashi ga tabete imas'. Watashi tabete imas'. Gohan o tabete imas'. Gohan tabete imas', watashi. Gohan—watashi ga tabete imas'.** A: **Anta—gohan o tabete imas' ne. Watashi mo, tabemashō. Nani tabemashō ka ne. Nani o tabemashō ka?** B: **Sō des' ne. Anta—nani o tabemas' ka? Nani tabemas' ka? Sakana o tabemas' ka? Niku o tabemas' ka?** A:

104

Sakana — tabemasen. Sakuban sakana
o tabemash'ta. Sore kara, byōki desh'ta
ne. Warui desh'ta. B: Nani ga warui
desh'ta ka? A: Sakana desh'ta. Sakana
ga warui desh'ta. B: Kono sakana—ii
des'. Watashi ga kaimash'ta. Kyō kaimash'ta ne. Dōzo tabete kudasai. A: Sā,
s'koshi tabemashō ne. Dōmo.

A: Koko de ne—dare ga nani o shimas'
ka? Dare ga mono o kaimas' ka? Dare
ga mono kaimas' ka? Dare ga kaimono
("shopping") shimas' ka? B: Jochū ga
mainichi no kaimono o shimas' ne. Tabemono ("food") o kaimas' ne, mainichi.
Soba no mise ("shop") e ikimas' ne.
Soko de kaimas'. A: Anta—nani o
shimas' ka, mainichi mainichi? B: Watashi des' ka? Watashi—mainichi shigoto
o shimas'. A: Donna shigoto des' ka?
Dō-yū shigoto o shimas' ka, anta? B:
Jimusho no shigoto des'. Watashi mainichi jimusho de shigoto o shimas'.

TIPS

In an English sentence, you know who
does what to whom by the order of the
words: "Tanaka looks at Nakamura"
means one thing and "Nakamura looks at
Tanaka" means another. But in Japanese,
the verb always comes at the end; you can

only say either **Tanaka san, Nakamura san, mite imas'** or **Nakamura san, Tanaka san, mite imas'.** Both of these sentences are vague; you can't tell who is looking and who is getting looked at. The order in which you place the two nouns (Tanaka and Nakamura) is all a matter of emphasis. You put first the one you have been talking or thinking about before—regardless whether it is the subject or the object. The first sentence (with Tanaka first) means either " Tanaka looks at NAKAMURA " or " NAKA-MURA looks at Tanaka "—the later position just shows additional emphasis in Japanese. The second sentence (with Nakamura first) means either " Nakamura looks at TANAKA " or " TANAKA looks at Nakamura." In order to help show who is the subject and who is the object, Japanese has two particles: **ga** for the subject, and **o** for the object. These are frequently used, even when you wouldn't have any doubt—in **Dare ga kimash'ta ka?** "Who came?" the **ga** tells you very little you don't already know without it. Notice that you can say either **Tanaka san ga Nakamura san o mite imas'** or **Nakamura san o Tanaka san ga mite imas'.** The difference is a slight shift in emphasis. After a verb, the particle **ga** means " but " or " and." Remember that each particle refers directly to the word preceding it, and is tacked right on to that word in pronunciation. Don't pause in front of a particle.

106

A : Who is eating ? Who is eating dinner ? Who is eating (his) dinner ? *B* : It's me. I am eating. I'm eating. I'm eating my dinner. I'm eating dinner, I am. Dinner—I'm the one that's eating it. *A* : You are eating dinner, aren't you. I think I'll eat too. What shall I eat now. What shall I eat ? *B* : Let's see. What will you have ? What'll you eat ? Will you eat fish ? Will you eat meat ? *A* : Fish—I won't have. I ate fish last night. And then I got sick. It was bad you see. *B* : What was bad ? *A* : It was the fish. The fish was bad. *B* : This fish is good. I bought it. I bought it today. Please eat some. *A* : Well, I'll eat a little then. Thank you.

A : Who does what around here ? Who buys things ? Who does the shopping ? *B* : The maid does the everyday shopping. She buys the food, you see, every day. She goes to a shop nearby. There she shops. *A* : What do you do all the time ? *B* : Me ? I work every day. *A* : What sort of work is it ? What kind of work do you do ? *B* : It's office work. I work in an office every day.

Lesson 25

A SENTENCE OPENER (*wa*)

PHRASES

Is there any bread?	**Pan ga arimas' ka?**
There isn't any bread.	**Pan wa—arimasen.**
What isn't there any of?	**Nani ga arimasen ka?**

It's BREAD there isn't any of.	Pan ga arimasen.
Who has some bread?	Dare ga pan ga arimas' ka?
Who has the bread?	Pan wa—dare ga arimas' ka?
How about fish—is there any?	Sakana wa—arimas' ka?
There ISN'T any fish, but there IS some meat.	Sakana wa arimasen ga, niku wa arimas'.
Today the weather's nice.	Kyō wa o-tenki ga ii des' ne.
What is this?	Kore wa nan des' ka?

PRACTICE

A: **Chotto! Negaimas'! Nē-san! Chotto!** Waitress: **Hai, hai. Sugu ikimas'. Nani o tabemas' ka?** A: **Sō des' ne. Nani ga arimas' ka?** W: **Sakana ga arimas'. Yasai ga arimas'.** A: **Niku wa arimasen ka?** W: **Arimas'. Niku wa arimas'. Bifuteki ga ("beefsteak") arimas' ne.** A: **Sō des' ka. Sā, bifuteki ne —bifuteki o motte kite kudasai. Sore kara yasai mo motte kite ne.** W: **Hai, hai. Sugu motte kimas'. Bifuteki wa, ōkii bifuteki des' ka, chiisai bifuteki des'**

ka. Ōkii bifuteki wa yon-hyaku en des'
ne. Chiisai bifuteki wa sam-byaku en
des'. A: Ōkii bifuteki ga ii deshō ne.
Ōkii bifuteki o motte kite kudasai. Sore
kara ne. W: Hai. A: Yasai wa—tak'san
motte kite ne. W: Hai, hai. Nani o
nomimas' ka? A: Miruku ga arimas' ka?
W: Arimasen, miruku wa. Biiru ga arimas'. Kōhii mo arimas'. Miruku wa
arimasen ne. Sumimasen. A: Kamaimasen. (" It makes no difference.") Biiru
wa, Amerika no des' ka, Nihon no des'
ka? W: Nihon no des'. A: Biiru ippon
motte kite kudasai ne. Biiru o ippon ne.
Biiru o nomimas'. W: Biiru des' ka?
Biiru o nomimas' ka? Biiru wa ima
nomimas' ka, gohan no ato de nomimas'
ka? A: Ima nomimas' ne. W: Hai, hai.
Sugu motte kimas', biiru wa. Sugu ato
de, bifuteki o motte kimas' ne. Chotto
matte kudasai.

Tips

The particle **wa** is a kind of sentence
opener—it tells you what you are going to
talk about. In earlier lessons, you often
started a sentence with a noun and then a
pause: **Kore—nan des' ka?** "What is
this?" The pause more or less corresponds
to the meaning of **wa** " as for ": **Kore wa**

nan des' ka? " As for this—what is it ?"
When you are making up a sentence, you
can pick out any part and put it at the
beginning (except the verb—that is always
at the end). The part at the beginning has
less emphasis than the parts which come
later ; to reduce the emphasis still further,
you can add **wa**. These differences of emphasis are rather subtle, and they seldom
show up clearly in the English translations.
Sometimes the English sentences suggest the
opposite : When we contrast two things in
English we stress the two things themselves,
not what is different about them : " TANAKA
is a Japanese, but BROWN IS an American."
The Japanese reduces the emphasis on the
two things in contrast so as to play up their
points of difference ; he does this with the
particle **wa** : **Tanaka san wa Nihon-jin des'
ga,** *Brown* **san wa Amerika-jin des' ne.**
Like the particle **mo, wa** can follow other
particles (**Tokyo made wa kisha desh'ta
ga, sore kara wa kuruma desh'ta.** " As
far as Tokyo it was by train, but from there
on it was by car."), but instead of following the subject or object particles, **wa** RE-
PLACES the **ga** or **o**. So you can take a
sentence like **Tanaka san ga Nakamura
san o mimash'ta** and change it to **Tanaka
san wa Nakamura san o mimash'ta.**
" Tanaka—he looked at Nakamura " or to
**Nakamura san wa Tanaka san ga mima-
sh'ta.** "Nakamura—Tanaka looked at him."

("TANAKA looked at Nakamura."). Notice
whether it is the subject or the object, or
whatever, the part with **wa** comes at (or
very near) the beginning of the sentence,
unless it is added as an afterthought after
the verb. Since **wa** is a device to shift emphasis somewhere away from the word in
front of it (playing up the rest of the sentence), you hardly ever find it after question
words like **dare** "who," **nani** "what," **doko**
"where," etc. When you ask **Dare kima-
sh'ta ka?** "Who came?" the thing you
are mainly interested in is "Who?" so the
appropriate particle is **ga**: **Dare ga kimash'ta ka?** The answer will also have **ga**
(Tanaka san ga kimash'ta.), because you
want to emphasize the new information you
are supplying. With negatives, the particle
wa is often appropriate, since you want to
play up the "NOT" idea: **Watashi wa
tabemasen.** "I—won't eat." **Sore wa kaimasen.** "That—I won't buy it." Frequently,
when there is no other topic around to use
as your sentence opener, you take the time
or place: **Kyō wa doko e ikimas' ka?**
"Where are you going today?" **Koko ni
wa benjo ga arimas' ka?** "Is there a
toilet here?"

A: Hey! Excuse me! Waitress! Hey! *Waitress*:
Yes, sir. I'm coming right away. What will you
have to eat? *A*: Let's see. What have you got?
W: We've got fish. We've got vegetables. *A*:
You don't have meat? *W*: We do have. We've

111

got meat. We've got beefsteak. *A*. You have? Well, then, bring me a steak. And then bring me some vegetables too. *W*: Yes, sir. I'll bring them right away. Do you want the large beefsteak, or the small? The large one is 400 Yen, the small one is 300. *A*: The large one would be good (*or* better), wouldn't it. Bring me a large one. And then, too... *W*: Yes. *A*: Bring lots of vegetables. *W*: Yes, sir. What will you have to drink? *A*: Have you got milk? *W*: We don't have, milk. We've got beer. We've got coffee too. We haven't got any milk. I'm sorry. *A*: That's all right. Is your beer American or Japanese? *W*: It's Japanese. *A*: Bring me a bottle of beer. One bottle of beer, see. I'll drink beer. *W*: Beer? You'll take beer? Will you have your beer now, or will you have it after the meal? *A*: I'll take it now. *W*: Yes, sir. I'll bring it right away, the beer. Right after, I'll bring the steak. Wait just a moment please.

Lesson 26

WHAT DID YOU SAY?

Phrases

What did you say?	Nan to iimash'ta ka?
What is this called in Japanese?	Kore wa nihongo de nan to iimas' ka?
How do you say it in Japanese?	Nihongo de dō iimas' ka?
What is your name?	Namae wa nan to iimas' ka?

112

He said, "It is bad."	"Warui des'" to iimash'ta.
He said that it was bad.	Warui to iimash'ta.
He said, "I'm going home."	"Kaerimas'" to iimash'ta.
He said he was going home.	Kaeru to iimash'ta.
He said, "I have already seen it."	"Mō mimash'ta" to iimash'ta.
He said he had already seen it.	Mō mita to iimash'ta.
He said "Let's go."	"Ikimashō" to iimash'ta.
He suggested we go.	Ikō to iimash'ta.
He asked, "Have you eaten?"	"Tabemash'ta ka?" to kikimash'ta.
He asked if I had eaten.	Tabeta ka (to) kikimash'ta.
Who were you talking with?	Dare to hanash'te imash'ta ka?
Won't you come with me?	Watashi to issho-ni kimasen ka?
I bought books and pencils.	Hon to empitsu o kaimash'ta.
It is between Yokohama and Kamakura.	Yokohama to Kamakura no aida des' ne.

113

The chair is be-   **Isu wa tēburu to
tween the table   mado no aida ni
and the window.   arimas'.**

PRACTICE

A: **Anta wa, denwa o kakete imash'ta
ne. Dare to hanash'te imash'ta ka?** B:
**Tanaka san desh'ta ne. Tanaka san to
hanash'te imash'ta.** A: **Nan to itte imash'ta ka, Tanaka san wa?** B: **Koko e
kuru** (=**kimas'**) **to iimash'ta ñe.** A: **Sugu
kuru to iimash'ta ka?** B: **Ichi-jikan ato
de** ("in an hour") **kuru to iimash'ta.
Sono aida** ("meanwhile") **jimusho e iku**
(=**ikimas'**) **to iimash'ta. Sore kara koko
e kimas' ne. Issho ni gohan o tabeyō**
(=**tabemashō**) **to kare ga itte imash'ta
ga ne, ikaga des' ka?** ("How do you feel
about it?") A: **Sumimasen ga ne. Mae
ni** ("before," "earlier") **tomodachi to hanash'te imash'ta ga ne. Sono tomodachi to
taberu** (=**tabemas'**) **to, watashi ga iimash'ta.** B: **Sō des' ka? Sā, watashi wa
Tanaka san ni sō iimashō ne.** A: **Hai,
sō itte kudasai ne. Dōmo. Tanaka san
wa, doko ni imash'ta ka, denwa no toki
ne** ("when he phoned"). B: **Watashi
kikimash'ta ga, eki to jimusho no aida
ni ita** (=**imash'ta**) **to iimash'ta.**

114

TIPS

The particle **to** means something like "quote" or "(said) that ..."; you put it after a word or phrase you are quoting, before the verb which means "says," "asks" or the like. The quote is usually indirect, so the Japanese replaces his ordinary POLITE forms (**shimas', shimash'ta, shimashō**) with the corresponding PLAIN forms (**suru, sh'ta, shiyō**). You may find some of these plain forms confusing at first. If you want to use the polite forms in quoting, everyone will understand you. Japanese quote things a good deal more of the time than we do, and sometimes the quotation is just a grammatical device. You quote thoughts, for example: **Pan ga aru (=arimas') to omoimas'**. "I think there is some bread." **Ikō (=ikimashō) to omotte imash'ta.** "I was thinking that I'd go." or "I was thinking we ought to go." Sometimes a Japanese shows a sentence is a quote by ending it just with the particle **to,** or—more often—another particle with the same meaning **tte**: **Tanaka san kimas' tte?** "Did Tanaka say he was coming?" **Issho ni tabemashō tte.** "He suggested we eat together." **Tanaka san tte?** "Did you say your name was Tanaka?" **Nan tte?** "What (did you say)?" **Kore tte?** "You mean this?" Another meaning of the particle **to** is "with" or "and"; **hon to shimbun** means "the news-

115

paper with the book " or " the book and the newspaper." At the end of the phrase you tack on the appropriate particle to link it with the rest of the sentence: **Hon to shimbun ga arimas'**. " We have books and newspapers." **Hon to shimbun o yomimas'.** " We read books and newspapers." **Hon to shimbun wa — doko de kâimas' ka?** "Where do you buy books and newspapers?" The phrase **watashi to issho-ni** means " together with me," and it can be shortened to just **to** "with": **Watashi to kite kudasai.** " Please come with me."

A : You were on the phone, weren't you. Who were you talking to? *B*: It was Mr. Tanaka. I was talking with Mr. Tanaka. *A* : What did he have to say, Mr. Tanaka? *B* : He said he's coming here. *A* : Did he say he's coming right away? *B* : He said he's coming in an hour. He said he was going to the office meanwhile. After that he's coming here, you see. He was suggesting we have dinner together—how do you feel about it? *A* : I'm sorry but, you see, I was talking with a friend earlier. And I said I'd eat with him. *B* : You did? Well, I'll tell that to Mr. Tanaka. *A* : Yes, please tell him that. Thank you. Where was Mr. Tanaka when he phoned (just now)? *B* : I asked him, and he said he was between the station and his office.

Lesson 27
IS IT OR ISN'T IT?

PHRASES

Is it a *sushi* (pick-led-rice) shop?	Sushi-ya des' ka?
It is.	Sō des'.
It isn't.	Sō ja arimasen.
It's something different (from that).	Chigaimas'.
It isn't a *sushi* shop.	Sushi-ya ja arimasen.
It is a noodle shop.	Soba-ya des'.
Did you say it is a *sushi* shop?	Sushi-ya da to iimash'ta ka? Sushi-ya da tte? Sushi-ya des' tte?
He said it isn't.	Sō ja nai to iimash'ta ne. Sō ja nai tte ne. Chigau to iimash'ta ne. Chigau tte ne.
Was it American food (you had)	Sakuban yōshoku de-sh'ta ka?

117

last night?

It was.	Sō desh'ta. ⌈ta.
It wasn't.	Sō ja arimasen desh'-
It was something different.	Chigaimash'ta.

| Did you say it was American food? | ⎰ Yōshoku datta to ii-
mash'ta ka?
Yōshoku datta tte?
Yōshoku desh'ta tte? |

| He said it was. | ⎰ Sō datta to iimash'ta.
Sō datta tte.
Sō desh'ta tte. |

| He said it wasn't. | ⎰ Sō ja nakatta to ii-
mash'ta.
Sō ja nakatta tte.
Sō ja arimasen desh'-
ta tte.
Chigatta tte.
Chigaimash'ta tte. |

| Is it probably Japanese food? | Washoku deshō ka? |

| Did you say it is probably Japanese food? | ⎰ Washoku darō to ii-
mash'ta ka?
Washoku darō tte?
Washoku deshō tte? |

PRACTICE

Yamamoto: **Komban doko de tabemashō ka.** Tanaka: **Sō des' ne. Nakamura-ya**

118

to yū (= to iimas' "named") tokoro e ikō
to omotte imash'ta ga ne. Y: Nakamura-
ya tte? T: Sō des'. Ii tokoro da to,
tomodachi ga itte imash'ta ne. Sono
tomodachi wa sakuban soko de tabeta tte.
Y: Sō des' ka? Soko no tabemono wa
yōshoku desh'ta tte? T: Iie, sō ja arimasen. Washoku datta tte ne. Washoku
datta to itte imash'ta ga, anta washoku
s'ki deshō? Y: Mada tabemasen desh'ta.
T: Mada tabemasen desh'ta tte? Sā,
komban tabete kudasai ne, washoku wa.
Y: Ha, arigato, dōmo, Tanaka san. Tanaka san, dōmo arigato. T: Dō itashimash'te. Y: Nakamura-ya to yū tokoro
wa doko darō ka to kikimash'ta ka,
tomodachi ni? T: Hai, kikimash'ta. Eki
no soba da tte. Eki o deru tte ne (= demas' "come out of"). Sore kara migi
des' tte. Sugu wakaru (= wakarimas'
"understand [where it is]") to itte imash'ta
ne. Y: Densha de ikimas' ka? T: Chigaimas'. Y: Chigaimas' tte? Nan de
ikimas' ka? T: Chikatetsu ("subway")
des'.

TIPS

The negative form of des' is a phrase:
ja arimasen "it isn't." The plain past is
datta (= desh'ta "was"), the present da

119

(=des' "is"), and the suggestion form darō
(=deshō "probably is"). The plain negatives are ja nakatta (=ja arimasen desh'ta
"wasn't"), ja nai (=ja arimasen "isn't"),
and ja nai darō (=ja arimasen deshō
"probably isn't". The word nai is the
plain form of arimasen "there isn't any";
its past is nakatta (=arimasen desh'ta
"there wasn't any"), and the suggestion
form is nai darō (=arimasen deshō) "there
probably isn't any."

Yamamoto: Where shall we eat? *Tanaka*: Let's
see. I was thinking of going to a place called Nakamura-ya. *Y*: You say Nakamura-ya? *T*: That's
right. A friend was saying it's a good place. He
said he ate there last night. *Y*: Oh? Did he say
the food there was American? *T*: No, he didn't.
He said it was Japanese. He was saying it is Japanese—would you like Japanese food? *Y*: I haven't
eaten any yet. (" *Yamamoto*" *must be an alias!*)
T: You say you haven't eaten any yet? Well, eat
some tonight, Japanese food. *Y*: Well, thank you
very much, I will, Mr. Tanaka. Thank you very
much, Mr. Tanaka. *T*: Not at all. *Y*: Did you
ask where the place called Nakamura-ya is located?
(Did you ask) your friend? *T*: Yes, I asked. He
says it's near the station. He says when you
come out of the station, see. Then it's to the right,
he says. He was saying we'll find it right away.
Y: Are we going by streetcar? *T*: No. *Y*: You
say no? What are we going by? *T*: It's the subway.

Lesson 28

CAN YOU? PROBABLY

PHRASES

You must be an American.

I bet you are an American.

You are probably an American.

Anta wa Amerika-jin deshō ne.

You probably drink beer.

Biiru o nomu deshō ne.

You must have come from America.

Amerika kara kita deshō ne. (or ...ki-mash'ta deshō ne.)

Tanaka has probably already gone.

Tanaka san wa mō itta deshō. (or ... ikimash'ta deshō.)

I wonder where he's gone to.

Doko e itta deshō ka ne.

Can you write Japanese?

Nihongo o kaku koto ga dekimas' ka?

Can you speak Japanese?

Nihongo o hanasu koto ga dekimas' ka? (or Nihongo ga dekimas' ka?)

121

I can't speak English.	**Eigo dekimasen.** (or **Eigo wa dekimasen.** or **Eigo ga dekimasen.**)
Can you go a little faster?	**Mō s'koshi hayaku iku koto ga dekimas' ka?**
Can we eat here?	**Koko de taberu koto ga dekimas' ka?**

PRACTICE

A: **Anta wa Eigo ga dekimas' ka?** B: **Dekimasen. Anta wa Amerika-jin deshō ne. Nihongo wa dekimasen ka?** A: **S'koshi hanasu koto ga dekimas' ga ne. Kaku koto wa dekimasen. Anta wa Nihongo de kaku koto ga dekiru deshō ne. Gakkō e itta deshō ne. Soko de kaku koto o benkyō shita deshō ne.** B: **Sō des'. Gakkō e wa, hachi-nen ikimash'ta ne. Soko de yomu koto mo, kaku koto mo, yoku benkyō shimash'ta.**

A: **Anta wa as'ko no hoteru** ("hotel") **de sunde iru deshō ne** ("are living, I bet"). **Ii deshō ne, as'ko wa.** B: **Hai, sō des'. Soko de sunde imas'.** A: **Hoteru de taberu koto ga dekimas' ka?** B: **Dekimas'. Shokudō ga** ("dining room") **arimas' ne. Anta wa mita deshō. Shokudō o mita**

122

deshō. **Ōkii heya no shita ni arimas'.**
A: **Hai, mimash'ta. Sore kara** (" and
then ") **hoteru wa sentaku o suru deshō
ne** (" I bet they do your laundry "). B: **Hai
sō des'. Dorai-kuriiningu mo** (" dry cleaning too ") **shimas' ne.**

TIPS

Deshō means " probably is "; when you
put it after a verb it means " probably does,
did, or will do " or " does (did, will do), I
bet." The verb can be said in its polite
form (**shimas' deshō, shimash'ta deshō**),
but it is more common to use the plain
form (**suru deshō, sh'ta deshō**). The plain
present is also used in front of **koto** "fact "
or " act " in the expression **koto ga dekimas'** "can do." The literal meaning of
the expression is " the act is possible." So
Taberu koto ga dekimas' ka? means literally
" Is the eat act possible?" **Dekimas'** also
means " is produced "; **dekimash'ta** and
dekite imas' mean also " something is
ready." Notice that **koto** is used in other
expressions too, for example **kaku koto o
benkyō shimash'ta** " studied writing "
(literally " studied write act "). The plain
present form usually ends in **-u,** the plain
past in **-ta** (or **-da**). But the actual shapes
for particular verbs are somewhat complicated ; you will find it easiest to learn them
for each verb individually.

123

A : Can you talk English? B : I can't. You must be an American. Can't you talk Japanese? A : I can talk it a little, but you see... I can't write it. You can probably write in Japanese. You must have gone to school. I bet you studied writing there, didn't you. B : That's right. I went to school for 8 years. There I studied a lot, both reading and writing.

A : I bet you live in that hotel over there. That must be nice, over there. B : Yes, that's right. I live there. A : Can you eat in the hotel? B : Sure. There is a dining room, you see. You must have noticed it. You must have seen the dining room. It's below the large room. A : Yes, I saw it. And then I bet the hotel does your laundry too. B : Yes, they do. They do dry cleaning too.

Lesson 29

BECAUSE AND BUT

PHRASES

I'm not going because I haven't any money.	O-kane ga arimasen. Da kara ikimasen.
	O-kane ga arimasen kara, ikimasen.
	O-kane ga nai kara, ikimasen.
I have some, so it's OK (don't worry).	Watashi arimas'. Da kara daijōbu des'.
	Watashi arimas' kara, daijōbu des'.

124

It's OK, since he understands English.

Watashi aru kara, daijōbu des'.

Eigo ga wakarimas'. Da kara daijōbu des'.

Eigo ga wakarimas' kara, daijōbu des'.

Eigo ga wakaru kara, daijōbu des'.

It's no good because he doesn't understand English.

Eigo ga wakarimasen. Da kara, dame des'.

Eigo ga wakarimasen kara, dame des'.

Eigo ga wakaranai kara, dame des'.

I like it, so I'll buy it.

S'ki des'. Da kara, kaimas'.

S'ki des' kara, kaimas'.

S'ki da kara, kaimas'.

I like it, but I won't buy it.

S'ki des'. Keredomo, kaimasen.

S'ki des' Da kedo, kaimasen.

S'ki des' keredomo, kaimasen.

S'ki da keredomo, kaimasen.

125

PRACTICE

A: Watashi wa Amerika e ikō to omotte ita keredomo, Eigo ga wakaranai kara,
dame deshō ne. B: Daijōbu des'. Watashi ga issho ni iku kara, daijōbu des'.
A: Anta wa Eigo ga jōzu des' tte ne.
("They say your English is very good.")
B: Dō itashimash'te. Heta des' ("poor"
or "clumsy"). Heta da keredomo ne,
s'koshi dekiru kara, daijōbu des'. Yoku
yomu koto ga dekiru keredomo, ammari
("overly," "too much") hanasu koto ga dekimasen ne. A: Gakkō de benkyō shita
deshō ne. B: Hai, gakkō de wa, yomu
koto o benkyō sh'ta keredomo, hanasu
koto o benkyō shimasen desh'ta ne. A:
Hanasu koto wa muzukashii des' tte ne.
("It's hard to talk.") B: Hai, sō des' ga
ne, yomu koto wa yasashii des'. ("...it's
easy to read.") B: Nihongo wa chigaimas'
ne. Hanasu koto wa yasashii keredomo,
kaku koto wa muzukashii des' ne.

TIPS

To start a sentence off with "So..." or
"Because of that..." you use the expression
Da kara.... If you want to link the two
sentences together into one, with the first
sentence the reason for the second, you use
the particle **kara** after the final verb of the

first sentence. The verb can either remain in its polite form, or change to the plain form. To start off a sentence with " But..." or " However..." you use **Keredomo...** or **Da kedo....** If you want, you can link the two sentences together by using **keredomo (kedo)** as a particle after the final verb of the first sentence, which can be either polite or plain. Another way to say " However..." is **Sh'kashi....** Another way to link two sentences with a very weak meaning of "but" (sometimes " and ") is the particle **ga**, usually used with the polite form of the verb: **Watashi wa Amerika-jin des' ga, Tanaka san wa Nihon-jin des'.** "I am an American, but (*or* and) Tanaka is a Japanese."

A : I was thinking of going to America, but I don't understand English, so it wouldn't be any good, would it. *B* : Don't worry. I'll go with you, so it'll be OK. *A* : They say your English is very good. *B* : Not at all. It's poor. I'm poor at it, but I can talk a little, so it'll be all right. I can read well, but I can't talk too well. *A* : You must have studied it in school. *B* : Yes, I learned to read in school, but I didn't learn to talk. *A* : It's hard to talk, they say, isn't it. *B* : Yes, it is, but it's easy to read. *A* : Japanese is the opposite. isn't it. It's easy to talk, but it's hard to read.

127

Lesson 30

HOW TO BE EMPHATIC

PHRASES

There — what's that?	Sore sa—nan deshō ka?
It's raining!	Ame ga futte (i)ru sa.
I tell you it's raining—look.	Ame ga sa, futte (i)mas' ne. Mite kudasai yo.
It's raining (you say)?	Futte (i)ru tte?
The picnic's out isn't it.	Ensoku wa dame des' ne.
It's out all right!	Dame des' yo.
It's really coming down hard!	Hidoku sa, futte imas'
Well then, what ("how") the devil shall we do?	Suru to sa, dō shimashō ka ne?
Are there any good movies on?	Ii eiga ga arimas' ka?
There *is* a good movie.	Ii eiga sa, arimas' yo.
But—I haven't any money.	Sh'kashi ne, o-kane ga nai sa.

128

So, I can't go.　　Da kara sa, iku koto
　　　　　　　　　ga dekimasen.

Well, shall we stay　Suru to ne, uchi ni
home then?　　　imashō ka?

We don't have　Sh'kata ga nai sa.
much choice!

So let's look at　Da kara sa, terebi
television.　　　mimashō.

But it's raining, so　Da kedo sa, ame ga
the television　futte (i)ru kara sa,
won't be any　terebi mo dame
good either.　　des' yo.

PRACTICE

A: Kyō sa, tenki ga warui des' ne. B:
Sō ne. Hidoku futte (i)ru sa. Dame des'
yo. Mainichi mainichi, iya des' yo. ("...
it's annoying.") Ima sa, kaeru koto ga
dekimasen ne. A: Daijōbu des' yo. Mada
sa ("still") s'koshi okane ga arimas' yo.
Da kara sa, kuruma de kaerimashō ("...
let's go home by taxi"). B: Chotto sa.
Matte ne. Shimbun o kaimas' kara sa.
A: Kuruma arimas' yo! Kuruma ga sa
kimash'ta. Ato de sa, shimbun katte ne.
Ima ikimashō. B: Daijōbu des' yo. Mō
katta (=kaimash'ta) sa, shimbun wa. Sā,
ikimashō.

129

TIPS

The particle **ne** is frequently used as a kind of polite pause, either at the end of the sentence or in the middle. An emphatic substitute for **ne** is **sa**, which is very common in Eastern Japan, including Tokyo, and various other parts of the country. You do not hear it much in Western Japan, where people are generally more soft-spoken, and many of the Western Japanese consider **sa** rather rude. But young people are fond of it, since it gives their speech a certain vigor and assertiveness. The particle **yo** is another way to be emphatic, and it is heard all over the country, more commonly at the end of a sentence than in the middle. In place of **ne**, country men often use **na**, which gives a more vigorous, but less sophisticated flavor to their speech. You also use **na** (and plain forms) when talking to yourself. Women often use the particle **wa** at the end of a sentence to soften its boldness. In rapid, friendly speech, polite forms are often replaced by plain forms, but the plain form is usually followed by some particle of emphasis or politeness. In rapid speech the first vowel of **imas'** is lost in the expression **-te (i)mas'** "is doing."

A: Say, today the weather's terrible, isn't it. *B*: Yeah, isn't it. It's really coming down! It's awful. Day after day, I hate it. Now we can't get home, can we. *A*: That's OK. I've still got a little money. So let's go home by taxi. *B*: Just a second. Wait up. I want to buy a paper! *A*: I've got a cab! A taxi has come! Buy your paper later! Let's go now. *B*: It's OK—I've got it, the newspaper. Well, let's go.

PART IV

3000 Useful Japanese Words

NOTE: Verbs are given in both the polite present (**-mas'**) and the plain present (**-u**). Where these two forms would be at about the same place in alphabetical order, they are given together; when they are rather different in shape, you will find two entries. Occasionally a word is out of alphabetical order for convenience, but not more than a place or two. If you do not find the word you are looking for, glance up and down the page a bit. Note that f' is alphabetized as **fu**, ts' as **tsu**, s' as **su**, etc.; sh' is alphabetized as **shi**, and ch' as **chi**.

A

abekku a couple (on a date), a date
abunai dangerous
abura oil, fat, grease
agarimas', agaru goes up
agemas', ageru raises up; gives
aida interval; between; while
aimas' (au) meets; sees (a person)
ainiku unfortunately
aisatsu greeting
aite the other fellow (companion; adversary)
aitsu that one over there
ajā, ajappā well, I'll be...!
aji taste
aka-chan baby
akai red
akabō redcap
akambō baby
akarui bright, light
akemas', akeru opens; leaves empty
aki autumn, fall
akimas', aku is open; is empt
amai sweet
ame[1] rain
ame[2] candy
ami net
ammari too much, overly

ana hole

anata you

ane older sister

ani older brother

ano that (over there)   ⌈(one's anxieties)

anshin shimas' (suru) doesn't worry, relaxes

anta you

aoi blue; green

arai rough, coarse

araimas', arau washes   ⌈corrects

aratamemas', aratameru changes, alters,

arawaremas', arawareru appears, shows

are that one (over there)   ⌊up, comes out

ari ant

arigato (gozaimas') thank you

arimas', aru¹ there is; we've got

arimash'ta there was; we had

aru² a certain

arubaito a side job, a sideline

arui-wa or else, maybe

arukimas', aruku walks

asa morning

asai shallow

ase sweat

ashi foot; leg

asobi fun; a game; a visit

asobimas', asobu has fun; plays; visits

asoko, as'ko (that place) over there

atama head

atarashii new
atarimas', ataru hits, faces; applies; is
at(a)takai warm ⌊correct
atemas', ateru guesses; hits; sets aside,
  appropriates, designates; touches; ad-
atena address ⌊dresses
ato after(wards), later
atsui[1] hot
atsui[2] thick

atsumarimas', atsumaru meet. assemble
atsumemas', atsumeru collects. gathers
au (aimas') meets, sees (a person)
awasemas', awaseru puts together, combines
azarashi seal (*animal*)
azukemas', azukeru entrusts, checks, deposits

B

-ba place
baai, bawai situation, case, circumstance
bai double
baka fool, idiot, stupid
ban[1] guard, watch; number
ban[2] evening
basho place
basu 1. bus 2. bath
batā butter
Beikoku America

beni rouge
benjo toilet
benkyō study
benri handy, convenient
bentō (box) lunch
betsu separate, special, particular
bin bottle ; jar
bōi boy, waiter, steward, clerk
boku I, me (man speaking)
bokushi minister, pastor ; Reverend
bōshi hat
botan button
bōzu Buddhist monk or priest
bu part, division, section
budō grapes
budō-shu wine
bumpō grammar
bun part, portion, share ; state, status
bungo literary language
bunka culture
bunshō (written) sentence
buta pig
buta-niku pork
byōin hospital
byōki sick ; sickness

C

cha tea

chadai tip
chakku zipper
champon alternating, skipping back and forth, mixing one's drinks (as beer and
chi blood ⌊saké)
chichi[1] father
chichi[2] breasts; mother's milk
chigaimas', chigau is different; is wrong;
chihō area, region ⌊isn't like that
chiisai, chiisa-na little, small
chiizu cheese
chika subway; underground; basement
chikai near, close by
chika-michi short cut
chikki[1] check, receipt, stub
chikki[2] stick hair-grease
chikuonki phonograph
chippu tip
chiri geography
chiri-gami Japanese Kleenex and toilet paper
chizu map
chō[1] block of a city
chō[2] head, chief, leader
chōdai please; I (humbly) take
chokki vest
chokusetsu direct
chō-kyori long distance
chōsa examination, investigation, inquiry
Chōsen Korea

chotto just a little ; just a minute
chū middle , medium
chūgakkō middle school (junior high school)
chūgata medium-size (model)
Chūgoku China
chūi[1] attention
chūi[2] 1st lieutenant ; lieutenant j. g.
chūshin center

D

da (**des'**) is ; it is
da ga but
dai- big
dai-(ichi) number (one)
daiben bowel movement
daigaku college, university
daiji important, precious
daijōbu OK, all right ; safe and sound ; no need to worry
daiku carpenter
daitai in general, on the whole, approximately, almost
da kara (**sa**) and so ; therefore ; that's why
dakimas', **daku** holds in the arms
damarimas', **damaru** is silent ; shuts up
damashimas', **damasu** deceives
dambō heating (in a house)
dame no good, no use, won't do ; don't !

dandan gradually

danna (san) master of the house ; husband

dantai organization, group

dare who

dare ka somebody

dare mo everybody ; nobody

dashi soup-stock ⌈mails ; begins

dashimas', dasu puts out; produces; spends:

da tte but ⌈of)

de[1] (happening) at, in, on ; with, by (means

de[2] is and; being, its being; with (its being)

de gozaimas' = de

deguchi exit

dekigoto happening, accident

dekimas', dekiru can, is possible ; is produced ; is finished, ready

dekimono swelling, sore, boil, pimple

demas', deru goes out, comes out, leaves,

dembu buttocks, hips ⌊starts

de mo but, however, even so

dempō telegram

denki electricity ; lights

densha electric car (streetcar or elevated)

dentō 1. lamp, light, flashlight 2. tradition, convention

denwa telephone (call)

depāto department store ⌈starts

deru (demas') goes out, comes out, leaves,

desh'ta was ; it was

141

deshō probably, probably is, it probably is

des', da is; it is; it is a case of ...

de wa (=**ja**) well then; in that case; and so ; and now

dō how, why ; (in) what (way)

doa door

dochira which one

dochira ka either one of the two

dochira mo either one ; neither one ; both

Doitsu Germany

doitsu which one

dokimas' (**doku**) gets out of the way

doko where

doko ka somewhere

doko mo everywhere ; nowhere

doku[1] poison

doku[2] (**dokimas'**) gets out of the way

donna what kind of ⌈so much

dōmo 1. thank you 2. excuse me 3. ever

dono which

dore which one

doro mud

dorobō thief, robber

doru dollar

dō-sh'te why ; how

dotchi=**dochira**

dotera padded bathrobe

doyōbi Saturday

dōzo please

142

E

e picture
ē yes
ebi shrimp; lobster
eda branch
e-hagaki picture postcard
e-hon picture book
eiga (-kan) movie (theater)
Eigo English
Eikoku England
eisei hygiene, health, sanitation
eki railroad station
en Yen
empitsu pencil
enkai party
ensoku picnic, outing
entotsu chimney, smokestack
erabimas', erabu chooses, selects, elects
erai great, superior

F

fu an urban prefecture (Kyoto or Osaka)
fū appearance, air; way, fashion, manner
fuben inconvenient, unhandy
fuchūi carelessness
fuda label, tag, card, check

143

fude writing brush

fudōsan real estate

fūfu husband and wife, Mr. and Mrs.

fuhei discontent, grumbling

fuhō illegal

fui suddenly

fujin lady

fu-jiyū inconvenient ; needy ; weak

fukai, f'kai deep

fukimas', f'kimas' see fuku, f'ku

fukin, f'kin napkin, towel, cloth

fuku, f'ku[1] 1. blows 2. wipes

fuku, f'ku[2] clothes, suit, dress

fukuro, f'kuro bag, sack

fukushū, f'kushū review

fukuzatsu, f'kuzatsu complicated

fuman discontented, dissatisfied

fumei unknown, obscure

fumimas', fumu steps on

fun minute

funayoi seasick(ness)

fundoshi a loincloth, a jockstrap

fune boat

fun-iki atmosphere

Furansu France

furemas', fureru touches, comes in contact

furi manner, air, pretense

furimas', furu[1] precipitates (rains, snows)

furimas', furu[2] waves, shakes, wags

144

furo bath

furōnin vagabond, tramp

furoshiki, furosh'ki a cloth wrapper

furu second-hand

furui old

furyō bad, no good

fūryū elegant

fusagimas', fusagu stops up, closes, blocks

fusawashii suitable, worthy ; becoming

fusegimas', fusegu prevents ; defends, protects

fushigi strange ; wonderful ; suspicious

fusoku shortage, deficiency, scarcity

fusuma opaque sliding door

futa, f'ta lid

futari, f'tari two persons

futatsu, f'tatsu two; two years old; 2nd day

futo, f'to unexpectedly

futoi, f'toi fat, plump

futon, f'ton Japanese padded quilt

futsuka two days

fuyu winter

G

ga[1] SUBJECT PARTICLE (*shows the actor :* who does, what is)

ga[2] but ; and

gai damage, harm, injury

gaijin foreigner (usually American or European)

gaikō-kan diplomat

gaikoku abroad; foreign countries

Gaimu-shō Ministry of Foreign Affairs

gakkō school

gaku learning, study, science

gakumon knowledge, learning, education

gakusei, gak'sei student, schoolboy

gakusha, gak'sha scholar

gamaguchi purse, pocketbook, wallet

gaman shimas' is patient, puts up with

gaman dekimasen (dekinai) can't stand it

gan-yaku a pill

garasu glass

gasorin gasoline

gasorin-sutando (-s'tando) filling station

gasu, gas' gas

gasu-dai gas bill

gehin vulgar

gei arts, accomplishments; tricks, stunts

geijutsu art(s)

geisha a geisha girl

geki play, drama

gekijō theater

gekkyū monthly salary

gemmai unpolished rice

gemmitsu strict

gendai modern, up-to-date

gengo language

gen-in cause, origin, root

genki in good spirits, healthy, cheerful, vigorous

genkin, gen-nama cash, ready money

genshi(-bakudan) atom (bomb)

genzai the present (time)

genzō shimas' develops (film)

geppu monthly instalments

geri diarrhea

geri-dome anti-diarrhetic, paregoric

geshuku lodgings; board and room

-getsu month

getsuyōbi Monday

gikai the Japanese Diet (Congress)

gimon question, doubt

gimu duty, obligation

gin silver

ginkō bank

giri obligation, sense of obligation, honor

go 1. five 2. checkers

-go language

gofuku-ya dry goods store

gogatsu May

gogo P.M., afternoon

gohan cooked rice; meal; food

go-jū fifty

Gokigen yō! 1. Goodbye 2. Hello

goku very, exceedingly

Gomen kudasai! Hello—anybody home?

Gomen nasai. Excuse me.

147

gomi trash, rubbish, dust
gomu rubber
goran ... (you) look, see, try
Goshimpai naku! Don't worry about it.
go-yō your business
gozaimas'=arimas'
guai condition, shape, feelings (of health)
gumpuku military uniform
gun army, troops
gunjin soldier, military man
gunsō sergeant
guntai troops, army ┌D.A.C.
gunzoku civilian attached to the army,
gutai-teki concrete, substantial, tangible,
gūzen accidentally └material
gyaku opposite, contrary
gyofu fisherman
gyōgi behavior, manners
gyūniku beef
gyūnyū milk

H

ha tooth
haba width
habukimas', habuku cuts out, reduces,
hachi[1] eight └saves, eliminates, omits
hachi[2] bowl, basin
hachi[3] (**mitsu-bachi**) bee

148

hachi-jū eighty

hadaka naked

hadashi barefoot

hae housefly

hagaki postcard

hage bald

hageshii violent, severe

haha mother

hai[1] yes

hai[2] ashes

hai[3] cupful

haibyō TB

hai-iro gray

haikara fashionable, high-class

hairimas', hairu enters; is inside

haitte imas' is inside

haitatsu delivery

haiyū actor

hajimarimas', hajimaru it begins (starts)

hajime the beginning; in the beginning

hajimete for the first time

hajimemas', hajimeru begins (starts) it

Hajimemash'te. How do you do. (on being introduced)

hakari measuring scales

hakarimas', hakaru measures, weighs

hakimas' (haku) 1. vomits, spits out 2. sweeps 3. wears on feet

hakkiri plainly, clearly, distinctly

hakkō publication

hako box

hakobimas', hakobu carries, conveys

haku 1. vomits, spits out 2. sweeps 3. wears ⌊on feet

hama beach

hambun half

hamemas', hameru wears (on fingers)

ha-migaki dentifrice, toothpaste, tooth-han¹ half ⌊powder

han² a seal (to stamp one's name with)

hana¹ flower

hana² nose

hanabi fireworks

hanagata a star (in a theatrical production)

hanao thong (on geta) ⌈distant

hanaremas', hanareru separates, becomes

hanashi talk, story, tale

hanashimas', hanasu speaks, talks; lets loose, lets go, sets free

hane feather; wing

han-i scope, range

hantai opposite, contrary, reverse

hantō peninsula

happa leaf

hara¹ belly, stomach

hara² field ⌈shakes out

haraimas', harau 1. pays 2. brushes aside,

haremas', hareru 1. (weather) clears up

hari needle; hand (of clock) ⌊2. swells up

harimas', haru sticks on, pastes; spreads,
haru springtime ⌊stretches
hasami scissors, clippers
hashi[1] bridge
hashi[2] (o-hashi) chopsticks
hashigo ladder, stairs ·
hashirimas', hashiru runs
hasu oblique, slanting
hata flag
hatake field
hataki duster
hatakimas', hataku slap, beat; dust
hatarakimas', hataraku works
hato pigeon, dove
hatoba pier, wharf
hatsumei invention
hatsuon pronunciation
hattatsu development
hayai, hayaku fast, quick
hayarimas', hayaru is popular, is in fashion
hayashi[1] forest
hayashi[2] hash ⌈reasonable to expect
hazu is expected to; is supposed to; is
hazukashii ashamed
hazumimas', hazumu bounces back; cheers
hazuremas', hazureru gets disconnected,
 comes off, misses, fails
hazushimas', hazusu disconnects, takes off,
he flatulence ⌊leaves one's seat

151

hebi snake ⌜tranged
hedatarimas', hedataru is distant, is es-
hedatemas', hedateru separates them, es-
hedo vomit ⌊tranges them, gets them apart
hei wall, fence
heiki calm, composed, cool, indifferent
heikin average
heitai soldier
heiwa peace
heizei usually, ordinarily, generally
hekomimas', hekomu gets hollow, depressed
hema bungle, mess
hen[1] **(na)** strange, odd, queer
hen[2] vicinity, neighborhood
henji answer
henka change ⌜down, shortens, curtails
herashimas', he-rasu decreases, cuts it
heri border, edge ⌜dles
herimas', heru goes down, decreases, dwin-
heso navel, bellybutton
heta unskilful, poor, inexpert
heya room
hi[1] fire
hi[2] 1. day 2. sun
hibachi charcoal brazier
hibikimas', hibiku echoes, resounds
hidari left
hidoi severe, unreasonable, terrible
hidoku hard, cruelly, terribly

152

hiemas', hieru gets cold

higashi east

hige beard, mustache

higeki tragedy

hiji elbow

hijō emergency

hijō ni extremely

hikaku comparison

hikarimas', hikaru shines

hiki- VERB PREFIX ("pull and" or "take ⌐and")

hikidashi drawer

hiki-kaemasu, -kaeru exchanges, converts

hikimas' (hiku) pulls (out); draws; drags; catches; attracts; subtracts; deducts; looks up a word ⌐dence)

hikkoshimas', hikkosu moves (one's resi-

hikōjō airport

hikōki airplane

hikō-yūbin airmail

hikui low, short

hima time; leisure, spare time; furlough, leave; dismissal (of servant); slow (busi-

himitsu secret, mystery ⌊ness)

himo string, cord, tape, strap

hin quality; elegance, refinement, dignity

hinan blame, censure, reproach

hinerimas', hineru twists

hiniku sarcasm; sarcastic; cynical

hinshitsu quality

153

hi-oi awning, sunshade, blind ⌈takes

hipparimas', hipparu pulls, drags, tugs at,

hiragana the roundish Japanese letters

hirakimas', hiraku opens up

hirattai flat

Hirippin Philippines

hiroba a square, a plaza, an open space

hiroi wide, broad

hiroimas', hirou picks up

hiru daytime ; noon

hiru kara afternoon

hiru-ma daytime

hisashi-buri ni after a long time (of absence)

hitai forehead, brow

hitei shimas' denies

hito person, man

hito- one

hitori one person

hitoshii equal, identical, similar

hitotsu one ; one year old ; one and the same

hitsuji sheep

hitsuyō necessity, need ; necessary

hiya (o-hiya) cold water

hiyashimas', hiyasu cools it off; refrigerates

hiyō cost, expense

hiyori weather; conditions

hiza knee, lap

hizuke date

hō¹ alternative ; one (of two) ; direction, way

154

hō[2] law ; rule ; method

hōbi (go-hōbi) prize, reward

hōbō everywhere, all over, every which way

hodo extent ; limits ; moderation ; approximate time ; (not) so much as ; the more...

hodokimas', hodoku undoes, unties

hoka other, in addition to, other than

hoken insurance

hokkyoku North Pole, Arctic

hokori[1] pride, boast

hokori[2] dust

hoku- north-

hōkyū pay, salary

hombu central office

hōmen direction, quarter, district

homemas', homeru praises

hommono the real thing

hōmon call, visit

hon book

hon- main ; chief ; this ; the ; present

hondō the main route

hone bone

honki serious, earnest

honno a slight, just a little, a mere

honrai originally, from the start

hontō, honto true ; truth ; really

hon-yaku translation

hoppeta cheek

hoppō north

Hora! Huh?! What's that?! Look at that!
hora¹ cave
hora² trumpet-shell; exaggerration ⌜to
horemas', horeru falls in love, takes a fancy
hori ditch, moat
horidashi-mono a bargain, a real find
hōritsu law
horiwari canal
horimas', horu digs, excavates
hoshi star
hoshi-(gaki) dried (persimmons)
hoshii is desired; desires, wants
hoshimas', hosu dries it
hoshō guarantee
hōsō (-kyoku) broadcast (station)
hosoi slender
hosu (hoshimas') dries it
hōtai bandage
hoteru hotel
Hotoke-sama Buddha
hotondo almost (all); almost all the time
hyaku hundred
hyaku-man million
hyakushō farmer
hyō table, schedule
hyōban reputation, fame
hyōgen expression (words)
hyōgu-ya paper-hanger, paper repairman
hyōjō expression (on face)

hyōjun standard
hyōjun-go standard Japanese
hyōmen surface
hyotto accidentally, by chance
hyotto sh'tara maybe, possibly
hyūzu fuse

I

i- medicine, doctoring
ian consolation; recreation
ichi[1] one
ichi[2] (**ichi-ba**) market, marketplace
ichi[3] position
ichiban number one; first; best; most
ichibu a part, portion
ichido one time
ichijirushii conspicuous, prominent, striking
ichijitsu one day; some day
ichimai a sheet; one
ido a well
ie a house
igai unexpected
igaku medicine, medical studies
...igo afterwards, from ... on
ii good
ii(-) (infinitive of **yū** "saying")
iie no
iimas', **yū** says

157

iimash'ta said
iin committee (member)
iin-kai committee
ii-wake explanation, excuse
iji temper, disposition
... **ijō** above, upwards of ...
ijō unusual
... **ika** below, less than ...
ika medical department
ikada raft
ikaga how (about it)?
ikagawashii suspicious, questionable, shady
ikari anger
ike pond
ikebana flower arrangement ⌈don't
ikemasen, ikenai it won't do; you mustn't;
iken opinion
iki breath
iki (na) smart, stylish
iki(-) (infinitive of **iku** "going")
ikioi vigor, energy, spirit
ikimas', iku goes
ikiru (ikite imas') lives, is alive
ik-ko one (piece)
iku (ikimas') goes
ikura how much
ikutsu how many; how old
ima now
imas', iru is, stays

imi meaning
imo potato
imōto younger sister
in seal, stamp
inai within
inaka country
inchiki fake, fraud
Indo India
Indoneshiya Indonesia
ine rice-plant
infure inflation
inki ink
inki (na) gloomy
inochi one's life
inori prayer
inshō impression
interi intellectual ; highbrow
inu dog
ippai 1. full 2. a cupful (glassful)
...irai since ...
Irasshai(mase)! Welcome!
irasshaimas', irassharu (someone honored)
  1. comes; 2. goes; 3. stays, is
ireba false teeth
iremas', ireru puts in, lets in
iriguchi entrance
irimas', iru¹ 1. is necessary; needs; wants
iru² (imas') is, stays ⌊2. roasts 3. shoots
iro color ; sex

isha doctor, physician
ishi[1] stone
ishi[2] will, intention
isogashii busy
isogimas', isogu hurries, rushes
issai all, everything, without exception
issaku-ban(-jitsu) night (day) before last
issho (ni) together with
isshō one's whole life
isshō-kemmei desperately; very hard
isshu a kind, a sort
isu chair
ita board, plank
itai painful, hurting
itami an ache, a pain
itashimas', itasu I (humbly) do
itazura mischief, prank
itchi agreement
ito thread, yarn; silk
itoko cousin
itoma =**hima**
itsu when
itsu-ka 1. 5 days; 5th day 2. sometime
itsutsu five
itsuwari falsehood, lie
ittai ...on earth, ...indeed
itte 1. going, goes and (gerund of **iku**) 2.
　=**yutte**: saying, says and (gerund of **yū**)
ittei fixed, settled, definite

ittō first, first class

iwa rock, crag

iwai celebration, party

iwayuru so-called, what you might call

iya no

iya (na) unpleasant; disagreeable; disliked

iyashii lowly, vulgar

iyo-iyo 1. at last 2. in fact 3. more and more

izen since, before, ago

J

ja, jā well, well then; in that case; now

ja arimasen (ja nai) it is not; it is not a case of

jagaimo Irish potatoes

jama interference, disturbance, hindrance, obstacle

jari gravel, pebbles

ji¹ a letter; a Chinese character

ji² hemorrhoids

ji³ land, ground; texture; fabric

-ji o'clock

jibiki dictionary

jibun oneself; myself; alone

jidai age, period, era, time

jidōsha automobile

jidō-teki automatic

jigyō enterprise, business

jihen incident, happening

jijō circumstances; conditions

jikan time ; hour
jika ni directly ; personally
jiki ni immediately ; soon
jikken experiment
jikkō performance ; practice ; realization
jiko accident
jiku axis, axle
jiman pride, boast
jimi plain, sober
jimu business, office work
jimuin office clerk
jimusho office
-jin person
jinkō population
jisatsu suicide
jishin¹ earthquake
jishin² self-confidence ⌈in fact, really
jissai actual conditions, reality ; in practice ;
jitensha bicycle
jitsu truth ; truly, really
jitsugyō business
jitsugyō-ka businessman
jitsuyō practical use, utility
jiyū freedom, free ; fluent, at ease
jōbu healthy, sturdy
jochū maid-servant
jōdan joke
jokyū waitress
jōriku disembarking, landing

162

jorō(-ya) whore(-house)

jōsha getting into a car, boarding

... joshi Madame, Miss, Mrs.

jōshiki common sense

jōtai condition, situation, circumstances

jōtō the best, first-rate

jōzu skilled, clever, good at

jū¹ ten

jū² gun

-jū throughout the...

jūbako nestling boxes, Chinese boxes

jūbun enough

jūdō jujitsu

jū-hachi eighteen

jū-ichi eleven

jūji a cross

jūku nineteen

jukugo a compound word

jū-man a hundred thousand

jumbi preparations

jun order, turn

jun (na) pure

jū-ni twelve ⌈is made to accord with

jun-jimas', -jiru applies correspondingly;

junjo order

junkan circulation; cycle

junsa policeman

jū-roku sixteen

jūsho residence

jūsu 1. orange soda pop 2. juice
jūtan rug, carpet
jūyō important
juzu beads

K

ka mosquito
... ka? QUESTION PARTICLE
... ka some ...., any ...
... ka... ... or ...
kabe wall
kabin flower vase
kabu stock (in a company)
kabushiki kaisha a corporation
kaburimas', kaburu wears on head
kachimas', katsu wins
kado (outside) corner
kaemas', kaeru[1] changes, exchanges
kaerimas', kaeru[2] goes home, goes back
kaeru[3] frog
kaeshimas', kaesu returns it
kaette contrary to expectations
kagaku science
kagami mirror
kage shade
kage-bōshi shadow
kagi key
kagimas', kagu smells it

kagiri limit, extent

kago basket

kagu furniture

kagu (kagimas') smells it

kai a meeting

-kai times, occasions

kaichū one's pocket

kaidan steps, stairs

kaidō an auditorium

kaigai overseas, abroad

kaigan seashore

kaigi meeting, conference

kaigun navy

kaii itchy

kaikan a public hall, a building

kaikei accounts

kaimas', kau[1] buys

kaimas', kau[2] raises, keeps (animals)

kaimono shopping

kaisha company

kaiwa conversation

kaji a fire

kajirimas', kajiru gnaws, nibbles

kakarimas', kakaru 1. it hangs 2. it takes, it requires 3. begins

kake 1. gambling; a bet 2. credit

kakemas', kakeru[1] 1. hangs it 2. telephones

kakemas', kakeru[2] bets

kakemas'. kakeru[3] runs, gallops

165

kakemas', kakeru multiplies

kaki[1] persimmon

kaki[2] oyster

kakimas', kaku writes; scratches

kakitome registered mail

kakomimas', kakomu surrounds

kaku writes; scratches

kakuremas', kakureru it hides

kakushimas', kakusu hides it

kama 1. pot; boiler 2. stove, oven, kiln
3. sickle

kamado kitchen range, stove

kamaimasen it makes no difference

kamban signboard

kami[1] hair (on the head)

kami[2] paper

kami-sama God; gods

kaminari thunder

kamisori razor

kamits'kimas', kamits'ku bites

kamo 1. wild duck 2. sucker, dupe

...ka mo shiremasen maybe ...

kampai a toast, "bottoms up"

kampan deck

kan a can

-kan for the interval of

kana Japanese syllabic writing

kanai my wife

kanamono hardware

kanarazu for sure
kanari fairly, rather
kanashii sad
kane money ; metal ; bell
kangae thought, idea, opinion
kangaemas', kangaeru thinks
kangofu nurse
kani crab
kanji[1] feeling
kanji[2] a Chinese character (letter)
kanjimas', kanjiru feels
kanjō bill ⌈concern
kankei connection, relationship, interest,
kan-kiri can opener
kankō sightseeing
kankōkyaku tourist
kanōsei possibility
kansha thanks, gratitude
kanshin[1] concern, interest
kanshin[2] **shimas'** admires
kanshō interference, meddling
kantan simple
kanzei customs duty
kanzen perfect
kanzō liver
kao face ; looks, a look ⌈shoplifts
kapparaimas', kapparau swipes, steals,
kara[1] shell, crust
kara[2] empty

...**kara** from ; since ; because, so

karada body

karai 1. spicy, hot, peppery 2. salty

karashi mustard

karasu crow

kare he, him

kare-ra they, them ⌐band

kare-shi lover, paramour ; boy friend ; hus-

karē curry

karē-raisu rice curry

kari temporary

karimas', kariru borrows

karimas', karu cuts, mows

karui light (of weight)

kasa umbrella

kasanarimas', kasanaru they pile up

kasanemas', kasaneru piles them up, puts
one on top of another

kasegimas', kasegu earns, works for (money)

kashi (o-kashi) cakes, sweets, pastry

kashima rooms for rent

kashimas' kasu lends

...**ka shira** I wonder if...

kashiya house for rent

kasu sediment, dregs

kasu (kashimas') lends

kasumi haze, mist

kata¹ shoulder

kata· form, shape, size, mold, pattern

kata person, honored person

-kata manner of doing, way

katachi form, shape

katagi respectable, steady, honest

katahō, kattappō one of a pair; the other one (of a pair)

katai hard; strong; upright; strict

katakana the squarish Japanese letters

katamari a lump

katamukimas', katamuku leans

katana sword

katarimas', kataru relates, tells

katawa cripple

katazukemas', katazukeru puts in order, straightens up, cleans up

katei[1] home, household, family

katei[2] hypothesis, supposition

katsu (kachimas') wins ⌈in deep fat

katsu a Japanese " cutlet "; anything fried

katsudō action, activity, movement, liveliness

katsugimas', katsugu carries on shoulders

katsuo (-bushi) a (dried) bonito fish

katsura a wig

katte[1] kitchen

katte[2] (ni) selfish(ly), as one wants to

kau[1] (kaimas') buys

kau[2] (kaimas') raises, keeps (animals)

kawa[1] river

kawa[2] skin

169

kawaii, kawairashii cute, loveable, darling
kawai-sō pitiful
kawakimas', kawaku gets dry
kawara tile
kawari change ; substitute
kawarimas', kawaru it changes; it takes
kawase a money order ⌊the place of
kaya mosquito net
kayōbi Tuesday
kayoimas', kayou commutes, goes back and forth, goes (regularly)
kayu rice-gruel, porridge
kayui itchy
kazan volcano
kazari (-mono) ornament, decoration
kazarimas', kazaru decorates
kaze 1. wind 2. a cold
kazoemas', kazoeru counts
kazoku family
kazu number
ke hair, wool, feathers
kechim-bo stingy person, skinflint
kedo = keredo(mo)
kega wound, injury
keiba horse racing
keiba-jō a racetrack
keibetsu despise
keiei management, operation
keikaku plan, scheme

170

keiken experience
kieki business conditions, prosperity, boom
keiko exercise, practice, drill
keirin bicycle race
keisan calculation, computation
keisatsu police
keishiki form, formality
keiyaku contract, agreement
keizai economics, finances
kēki a cake
kekka result; as a result (consequence)
kekkō 1. splendid; excellent 2. fairly well,
well enough; enough
Kekkō des'. No, thank you.
kekkon marriage
kekkyoku after all, in the long run
kembutsu sightseeing
kempei MP; shore patrol
kempō constitution
kemuri smoke
ken a Japanese prefecture (like a state)
kenchiku construction; architecture
kencho the prefectural government (office)
kenka quarrel
kenkō health
kenkyū research, study ⌈check-up
kensa, kensatsu inspection, examination,
ken-yaku economy, thrift, economizing
ke-orimono woolen goods

keredo(mo) however, though, but
kerimas', keru kicks
keshiki scenery, view
keshimas', kesu puts out; turns off; erases
keshō cosmetics, make-up
keshō-shitsu ladies lounge
kessan settling accounts
kesseki absent
kesshin determination, resolution
kesu (keshimas') puts out; turns off; erases
kettei determination, decision
ketten flaw, defect
ki¹ spirit; feeling; mind, heart
ki² tree; wood
kibishii strict, severe
kibō hope
kibun feeling, mood
kichi military base
ki-chigai mad, insane
kichin-to punctual; precise; neat
kido entrance gate, wicket
kiemas', kieru is extinguished, goes out; fades, vanishes
ki-iro yellow
ki-ito raw silk
kiji¹ article, news item
kiji² pheasant
kikai¹ chance, opportunity
kikai² machine, machinery
kikan engine; instrument; agency

172

kikasemas', **kikaseru** lets someone hear,
kiken danger, peril ⌊tells, informs
kiki-me ga arimas' is effective
kikimas', **kiku** listens, hears; obeys; asks;
kikō climate ⌊is effective, works
kikoemas', **kikoeru** can be heard, can hear
kiku (kikimas') listens, hears; obeys; asks;
kiku chrysanthemum ⌊is effective, works
kimarimas', **kimaru** is settled, is arranged
kimas'[1], **kuru** comes
kimas[2], **kiru** wears
kimben industrious, hardworking
kime grain, texture
kimemas', **kimeru** settles, arranges
kimi[1] you
kimi[2] feeling, sensation
kim-makie gold lacquer
kimo liver
kimochi feeling, sensation
kimono clothes; a kimono
kimpatsu blond
kimyō strange, peculiar
kin gold
kina quinine
kinen commemoration
kinem-bi anniversary
Kin-en No Smoking
kingyo goldfish
kinjo neighborhood, vicinity

173

kinō yesterday
ki-no-doku pitiful, pitiable
kinoko mushrooms
kinshi prohibition, ban
kinu silk
kin-yōbi Friday
kin-yū finance
kinzoku metal
kioku memory
kippu ticket
kirai is disliked; dislikes
kire a piece, a cut
kirei pretty; clean ⌜3. breaks down
kiremas', kireru 1. cuts (well) 2. runs out
kireme a gap, a break, a pause
kiri[1] fog, mist
kiri[2] a hole-punch, an awl, a drill
kiri[3] paulownia (tree or wood)
...(k)kiri only, just
kirimas', kiru cuts
kiritsu discipline ⌜4. kiloliter
kiro 1. kilogram 2. kilometer 3. kilowatt
kiroku record
kiru[1] (**kirimas'**) cuts
kiru[2] (**kimas'**) puts on, wears
kiryō personal appearance, looks; ability
kisen steamship
kisetsu season
kisha[1] railroad train

kisha [2] newspaperman, reporter
kishi shore, coast, bank
kishukusha dormitory, boarding house
kisoku rule, regulation
kissa-ten a tearoom
kita [1] north
kita [2] came (past tense of **kuru**) ; wore (past
kitanai dirty   [tense of **kiru**)
kite coming, comes and (gerund of **kuru**);
  wearing, wears and (gerund of **kiru**)
kitsui 1. tight 2. severe 3. bold
kitsune fox
kitte stamp
kitto no doubt, surely
kiwa brink, edge
kiwadoi dangerous, delicate, ticklish
kiwamarimas', kiwamaru comes to an end ;
  gets carried to extremes
kiwamemas', kiwameru carries to extremes ; investigates thoroughly
kiwamete extremely   [notches, nicks
kizamimas', kizamu chops fine ; carves ;
kizashi symptoms, signs, indications
kizu wound ; crack, flaw ; fault, defect
kizu-ato scar
ko child ; person
kō [1] this way, so, like this
kō [2] incense
kōba factory

kobamimas', kobamu refuses, rejects; opposes, resists
kōban police box
koboshimas', kobosu spills
kobu bump, knob, swelling
kobun henchman, subordinate, follower
kobune small boat
kobushi fist
kōcha black tea
kochira 1. here, this way 2. this one 3. me, I; us, we
kodai ancient times
kōdō[1] highway
kōdō[2] action, behavior
kodomo child ; boy
koe voice ; cry
kōen[1] public park
kōen[2] lecture
kōen[3] support
kōfu workman
kōfuku happiness
kōfun excitement
kōgai suburbs
kogashimas', kogasu scorches
kogata small-size (model)
kōgeki attack
kōgi lecture
kogimas', kogu rows
kogitte check
kōgo spoken language, colloquial
Kōgō sama the Empress

176

kogoe low voice, whisper
kogoto scolding
kogu (kogimas') rows
kōgyō industry
kōhei fair, impartial
kōhii coffee ; **-ten, -ya** coffeeshop
koi[1] carp (fish)
koi[2] love
koi[3] request
kōi goodwill
koibito sweetheart
koitsu this one
kōji construction work
kojiki beggar
kojin individual
kōjitsu excuse, pretext
kōkai public
kōkan exchange
koke moss
kōkishin curiosity, inquisitiveness
kokkai assembly, parliament, congress, Diet
kokkei amusing, funny
kokku cook
koko here, this place
kokonotsu nine
kokonoka 9 days ; the 9th day
kōkoku advertisement
kokoro mind, heart, spirit, feeling
kokoro-mochi feelings, spirit, mood

kokorozuke tip, gratuity

kokuban blackboard

kokubō national defense ⎡elevated)

Kokuden Government Electric (the Tokyo

kokujin negro

kokumin a people, a nation

kokunai internal, domestic, inland

kokuritsu national, government-run

kokusai international

kokuseki nationality

kokyō hometown, birthplace

kokyū respiration, breathing

koma a toy top

komakai 1. fine, small 2. detailed, exact
3. thrifty 4. small change

komarimas', komaru gets perplexed, embar-
komban tonight ⎣rassed, is at a loss

Komban wa. Good evening.

kombō club, billy-club, bludgeon

kombu (kind of seaweed)

kome rice

komi-itta complicated, intricate, elaborate

komori babysitter

kōmori 1. bat 2. umbrella

kompon foundation, basis ⎡curs

kōmurimas', kōmuru sustains, suffers, in-
kon dark blue

kona powder ; flour

kona-gusuri powdered medicine

178

konashimas', konasu powders; digests
kondo this time; next time
kongetsu this month
kongo from now on, in the future
konkūru prize contest
konna such a
konnan difficulty, trouble, hardship
Konnichi wa. Good afternoon. (Hello.)
kono this
kono-aida lately
konomimas', konomu likes, is fond of, pre-
kon-yaku engagement (to be married)
konzatsu confusion, jumble, disorder
koppu a glass, a cup
koraemas', koraeru 1. stands, bears 2. con-
kore this one ⌊trols, restrains, represses
kore-ra these
kōri[1] ice
kōri[2] baggage
kōritsu public, municipal
korogarimas', korogaru rolls, tumbles
koroshimas', korosu kills
koruku(-nuki) cork(-screw)
kōryo consideration, reflection
kōsa-ten an intersection (of streets)
kōsai social relations, company
koshi hips
koshi-kakemas', -kakeru sits down
koshimaki loincloth; petticoat

179

koshimas', kosu goes over ; exceeds

koshiraemas', koshiraeru makes, builds

koshō[1] 1. damage, something wrong 2. hindrance, impediment

koshō[2] pepper

kōshō negotiations ; connections

kōshū the public, the masses

...**koso** indeed (it is ...)

kosu (koshimas') goes over ; exceeds

kōsui perfume

kosurimas', kosuru rub, scrape

kotaemas', kotaeru answers

Kōtaishi sama the Crown Prince

kotchi = kochira

koto thing, matter ; fact ; case ; experience
...(**suru**) **koto ga aru** does do it ; does
it sometimes ; ...(**suru**) **koto ga nai**
never does it ; ...(**sh'ta**) **koto ga aru** has
done it ; ...(**sh'ta**) **koto ga nai** has never
done it

kotoba 1. word, words ; sentence (spoken)
2. speech 3. language

kotonarimas', kotonaru is different, differs

koto-ni especially ; moreover, what is more

kotoshi this year

kotowarimas', kotowaru 1. refuses, declines, begs off 2. makes excuses

kotowaza a proverb   ⌜one)

kotozuke, kotozute a message (for some-

kōtsū communication ; traffic

kottō-hin curios, antiques
kowai 1. afraid ; frightful, 2. terrific, swell
kowaremas', kowareru it breaks
kowashimas', kowasu breaks it
koya hut, shed
koyama hill
koyōji toothpick
kō yū this sort of, such
kōzan a mine
kozara saucer
kōzen open(ly), public(ly)
kozuchi a small hammer
kozukai[1] janitor ; attendant ; servant
kozukai[2] pin money, pocket money
kozutsumi package, parcel
ku[1] nine
ku[2] a ward (in a city) ⌈deals (cards)
kubarimas', kubaru distributes, allots ;
kubetsu difference ; discrimination
kubi neck
kubomi hollow, dent, depression
kuchi 1. mouth 2. words, speech 3. entrance ; hole, opening 4. cork, stopper
kuchi-beni lipstick ⌊5. job opening
kuchimas', kuchiru rots, decays
kuda pipe, tube
kudakemas', kudakeru it breaks, it smashes
kudakimas', kudaku breaks it, smashes it
kudamono fruit

181

kudari down, going down; descent

kudarimas', kudaru comes (goes) down; ...kudasai please ⌊falls, drops

kudasaimas', kudasaru gives; does the favor of

kudashi a purgative, a laxitive; a vermifuge

kudoi 1. long-winded, dull 2. thick, greasy

kufū device, scheme

kugatsu September

kugi nail

kugiri punctuation

kūgun air force

kui post, stake, pile

kuimas', kuu eats

kuji a lot (in a lottery)

kujira whale

kuki stalk, stem

kūki air

kuma bear

kumi a set, suit, pack; a class, band, com-

kumiai association, guild, union ⌊pany

kumiawase assortment, mixture

kumimas' kumu ladles, scoops up; considers, sympathize

kumitate structure, set-up, organization,

kumo¹ cloud ⌊frame-work

kumo² spider

kumorimas', kumoru gets cloudy

...**kun** young Mr. ...

kuni 1. country 2. native place, home area

kura[1] saddle

kura[2] warehouse, storeroom, cellar

kurabemas', kuraberu compares, contrasts

kurabu club

kurai[1] dark, gloomy

kurai[2] 1. grade, rank 2. situation; fix; as much as; to the extent; about, approximately

kurashimas', kurasu lives, gets by, makes a living

kurasu class

kuremas', kureru[1] gives; does the favor of

kuremas', kureru[2] gets dark

kuri chestnut

kuriimu cream

kuriiningu cleaning

kurimas', kuru winds, reels

Kurisumasu Christmas

kurō difficulties, hardships

kuroi black

kurōto expert, professional

kuru[1] (**kimas'**) comes

kuru[2] (**kurimas'**) winds, reels

kuruimas', kuruu goes mad, insane; gets warped; gets out of order

kuruma car; taxi; vehicle

kurushii painful; hard, heavy

kusa, k'sa grass, weed

kusai, k'sai smelly, stinking; fishy, questionable

kusari, k'sari chain
kusarimas', kusaru goes bad, rots, decays
kuse, k'se a habit
kushami, k'shami a sneeze
kushi 1. a comb 2. a skewer, a spit
kuso, k'so dung, excrement
kusugurimas', kusuguru tickles
kusuguttai ticklish
kusuri, k'suri medicine
kusuri-ya, k'suri-ya drugstore
kutabiremas', kutabireru gets tired
kutsu shoes
kutsu-bera shoehorn
kutsu-himo shoelace
kutsu-migaki shoeshine
kutsu-naoshi shoe-repairman
kutsu-shita, kutsu-sh'ta socks
kuttsukimas', kuttsuku sticks to
kuu (kuimas') eats ; bites
kuwa¹ hoe
kuwa² mulberry
kuwaemas', kuwaeru adds ; imposes
kuwashii detailed
kuzu waste, trash, rags
kuzushimas', kuzusu 1. cashes, changes, breaks (into small money) 2. breaks down, demolishes 3. simplifies
kyabarē cabaret, nightclub
kyabetsu cabbage

kyaku (o-kyaku) visitor, guest, customer
kyandē candy
kyarameru caramels
kyatsu = **koitsu**
kyō today
kyōdai brothers and sisters ; brother ; sister
kyōdō union, cooperation, joint
kyōgi[1] game, match, contest
kyōgi[2] conference, discussion
kyōiku education
kyōju professor
kyōkai church
kyoku office, bureau
kyokuba circus
kyokutō Far East
kyōmi interest
kyonen last year
kyori distance
Kyōsan-shugi(-shugisha) Communism, (-ist)
kyōshi teacher, instructor, tutor
kyōshitsu classroom, schoolroom
kyōsō competition, rivalry, contest
kyōtsū common, general
kyōyō[1] for common use, for public use
kyōyō[2] culture, education, refinement
kyū class, grade
kyūji waiter, waitress, steward, office-boy
kyūkō express (train, etc)
kyūri cucumber

185

kyūyo compensation, allowance, grant

M

ma room ; space ; time ; leisure

mā well ; I should say ; perhaps

machi town

machigai mistake

machimas', matsu waits for

mada (not) yet ; still

madara spots, spotted, polka dots

...made until ; as far as ; to

mado window

mae front ; in front of ; before

magarimas', magaru 1. turns, goes around 2. it bends, curves

magemas', mageru bends it, curves it

mago grandchild

mahi paralysis

mai- each

maiasa every morning

maiban every night

maido every time

maigo lost ; a lost child

mainen every year

mainichi every day ; all the time

mairimas', mairu 1. I come, I go 2. visits, calls on 3. is defeated, loses (a game, etc.)

maisō burial   ⌊4. is floored, stumped

Maitta ! You've got me !

majime serious, sober

majirimas', majiru mixes

majiwarimas', majiwaru associates with

makasemas', makaseru entrust with, leaves
   in one's hands

makashimas', makasu 1. beats down the
price 2. defeats

makemas', makeru 1. comes down on the
   price 2. loses, is defeated 3. is inferior

maki¹ firewood

maki² a roll ; a volume

maki-e raised lacquer

makimas'. maku rolls up ; winds ; wraps

makoto sincere ; faithful ; true ; genuine

makura pillow

... mama as it is ; as one wants

mame¹ beans

mame² blister, corn, bunion

mamorimas', mamoru defends, protects

man 10,000

man- fully

mane imitation

manekimas', maneku invites

manga cartoon, comics

man-ichi if by any chance

man-in full (of people)

mannaka the very middle

mannenhitsu fountain pen

Manshū Manchuria

187

manukaremas', manukareru escape from, be exempt from

manzai cross-talk comedy

mare rare

mari ball

maru circle, ring : zero

maru- fully

maru de perfectly, completely

marui round

masarimas', masaru surpasses, is superior

machimas', matsu waits for

massaka-sama head over heels

massugu straight

masu (mashimas') increases, raises, swells

mata¹ again ; moreover

mata² groin ; crotch

mata-wa or, or else ; also

matchi match

mato aim, target ⌈ranged, finished

matomarimas', matomaru is settled, ar-

matomemas', matomeru settles, arranges

matsu¹ pine tree

matsu² (machimas') waits for

matsuri a festival

mattaku quite, completely

mawarimas', mawaru goes around

mawashimas', mawasu turns around, passes around ⌈gets perplexed

mayoimas', mayou gets lost ; gets dazed ;

mayu 1. eyebrows 2. cocoon
mazu first of all, before anything else
mazui 1. untasty 2. awkward, poor 3. in- ⌐advisable 4. ugly
mazushii poor, needy
me 1. eye 2. bud
-me -th (**itsutu-me** "5th") ⌐order
mechamecha in pieces, all confused, in dis-
medetai 1. auspicious, happy 2. simple- ⌐minded
megane eyeglasses
mei niece ⌐tion, a famous product
meibutsu a local speciality, a special attrac-
meijin expert
meirei order, command
meishi calling card
meishi-ire calling card case
meiwaku trouble, annoyance
meiyo prestige, honor, glory
mekata weight
mekura blind
men[1] mask ; surface ; front
men[2] cotton
mendō trouble, difficulty, nuisance
menkai interview, meeting
meriyasu knitted goods
meshi cooked rice ; a meal ⌐drinks
meshiagarimas', meshiagaru 1. eats 2.
meshimas', mesu in formal speech can replace such verbs as *kimas'* (wears), *tabemas'* (eats), *nomimas'* (drinks), etc.

189

meshitsukai servant
me-tsuki a look (in one's eyes)
metta reckless, rash
metta ni+NEGATIVE VERB seldom
mezamashi (-dokei) alarm clock
mezurashii rare, uncommon, novel, curious
mi 1. fruit, nut 2. body
mi(-) INFINITIVE OF *miru* (seeing)
mibun social standing
miburi gesture, movement
michi street, road
michimas', michiru is complete, is full
midare disorder
midashimas', midasu throws into disorder
midori green ⌐ 2. shows up, comes
miemas', mieru 1. is visible, can be seen
migakimas', migaku polishes, shines
migi right
migoto splendid, beautiful
migurushii unseemly, unsightly
mihon a sample
mijikai short (not long)
mikan tangerine ⌐point
mikata 1. a friend, an accomplice 2. a view-
mikka 3 days; 3rd day ⌐3. opinion
mikomi 1. promise, hope 2. expectation
mimai a visit (especially of sympathy, etc.)
mimas', miru sees, looks; tries doing
mimi ear

mimi-wa earring
mina-san you all, everybody
minami south
mine peak, summit
minkan the people ; civilians ; civil
mino straw raincoat
minori crop, harvest
minshu-shugi democracy
minshū the masses, the people
min-yō folk song, ballad
minzoku race
mirin sweet saké
miru (mimas') sees, looks ; tries doing
miruku milk
mise store, shop
misemas', miseru shows
misemono exhibition, exhibit
mishin sewing machine
miso bean paste
misu bamboo blind
mitashimas', mitasu fills up, satisfies
mitomemas', mitomeru recognizes, admits
mitsukarimas', mitsukaru is found, dis-
   covered
mitsukemas', mitsukeru finds, discovers
mittsu three
miukemas', miukeru observes, happens to
miya a Shinto shrine   ⌊see
miyage a present, a souvenir

miyako capital, city

mizo drain, ditch

mizu (cold) water

mizuumi a lake

...mo also, too

...mo ...mo both...and...; neither... nor...

mō 1. already ; now 2. more

mochi rice cake

mochimas', motsu has, holds, carries

mochiron of course

modoshimas', modosu 1. vomits 2. sends back, returns

mohan model, pattern

moji letter, character, writing

mōkemas', mōkeru[1] makes money, profits

mōkemas', mōkeru[2] prepares, sets up

Mōko Mongolia

mokuhan woodblock print

mokuhyō target, goal

mokuroku catalog, list, table, inventory

mokutan charcoal

mokuteki aim, objective, purpose

mokuyōbi Thursday

mokuyoku bathing

momen cotton

momiji 1. maples 2. autumn leaves

momimas', momu massages; rubs; pounds on

momo 1. peach 2. hip, thigh

mon[1] family crest

mon[2] gate

mondai question, problem, topic
mon(o) 1. thing 2. person
... (sh'ta) mon(o) des' used to...
... mono because
mono- (emphatic prefix with adjectives)
monogatari a tale, a legend
monozuki curious, inquisitive
moppara principally, chiefly
moraimas', morau receives, gets ; has someone do for one
morashimas', morasu lets leak ; reveals
moremas', moreru leaks out ; is omitted
mori woods, forest
morimas', moru piles it up, accumulates it
moroi brittle, frail
mōru lace
moshi if
moshi moshi! hello! hey! say!
mōshikomi application
mōshimas', mōsu 1. I say 2. I do
moto 1. origin, source 2. (at the) foot (of)
motomemas', motomeru 1. wants, looks for
  2. asks for 3. buys, gets
moto-yori from the beginning ; by nature
motozukimas', motozuku is based on ;
  conforms to
motsu (mochimas') has, holds, carries
mottai-nai 1. is undeserving 2. it is waste-
motte ikimas' (iku) takes   [ful

193

motte imas' (iru) has. holds
motte kimas' (kuru) brings
motto more, still more; longer
motto-mo 1. most, exceedingly 2. indeed, of course 3. but, however
moyō pattern
mucha unreasonable; reckless; disorderly
muchi a whip
muchū trance, ecstasy
muda futile, no good, wasteful; useless
mudan de without notice, without permission
mugi grain; wheat, barley
mugiwara straw
mugoi cruel, brutal
muika 6 days; the 6th day
mujaki naive, innocent, unsophisticated
mujō heartless
mujun inconsistent; contradiction
mukaemas', mukaeru meets; welcomes; invites
mukaimas', mukau opposes; heads for
mukashi ancient times
mukimas', muku 1. faces 2. skins, pares
muko son-in-law; bridegroom
mukō opposite, across the way; over there (in America, etc.)
mukuimas', mukuiru repays; compensates
mumei nameless, anonymous
munashii empty; futile, in vain
mune[1] chest, breast; heart, mind
mune[2] purport, effect, intent

194

mura village

mure group, throng, flock

muri (shimas') (is) unreasonable, violent; overdoes; asking too much

muryō free of charge

mushi insect; worm

mushi-atsui muggy, close, sultry, humid

mushi-ba decayed tooth

mushi-kudashi vermifuge, worm remedy

mushimas', musu steams; is sultry, humid

musubimas', musubu ties; ties up, winds

musuko, mus'ko son ⌊up; wears a tie

musume daughter; girl

muttsu six ⌈ness

muyō unnecessary; useless; having no busi-

muzukashii hard, difficult

muzumuzu itchy, crawly, creepy

myō strange, queer

myōgonichi day after tomorrow

myōnichi tomorrow

N

n'=no

na¹ name

na² greens, vegetables

...na ! isn't it, don't-you-know, you see

nabe pan, pot

nademas' naderu soothes, pets

nae seedling
nagai, nagaku long
...-nagara while ....-ing
nagaremas', nagareru flows
nagashi kitchen sink
nagashimas', nagasu lets flow
nagaya tenement house
nagekimas', nageku weeps, moans, laments
nagemas', nageru throws
nagurimas', naguru knock, beat, strike
nagusame comfort, consolation
nagusami amusement, entertainment
nai (arimasen) there is no..., has no ..., lacks
naichi inside the country, inland, internal
naifu knife ⌈approximately
naigai inside and out; home and abroad;
naikaku a government cabinet
naka 1. inside, in 2. relations, terms (be-
nakama friend, pal ⌊tween people)
nakanaka extremely (long, hard, bad, etc.),
  more than one might expect
...-nakereba unless
...-nakereba narimasen must, has to
nakimas', naku weeps; cries; makes an
naku(te) without ⌊animal sound
nama 1. raw, uncooked; fresh 2. hard cash
namae name
namaiki impertinent
namakemas', namakeru idles, is lazy

196

namari 1. lead (metal) 2. dialect, accent
Nambei South America
namboku north and south
nambu the south, the southern part
namemas', nameru licks, tastes
nami[1] ordinary, common, average
nami[2] wave
namida tear
nana(tsu) seven   ⌈agonal
naname slanting, oblique, at an angle, di-
nan(i) what
nan-, nam- how many...
nan dai = nan des' ka what is it
nan de mo anything at all
nanibun anyway, anyhow   ⌈don't want to
nan-nara if you prefer, if you like; if you
nan no what (kind of); of what
nanoka 7 days; the 7th day
nao still more; moreover   ⌈cured, fixed
naorimas', naoru is corrected, repaired,
naoshimas', naosu corrects, repairs, cures,
... nara if   ⌊fixes
narabemas', naraberu arranges, lines them
  up   ⌈themselves
narabimas', narabu they line up, arrange
naraimas', narau learns
narashimas', narasu 1. smoothes, averages
  2. domesticates, tames 3. sounds, rings it
naremas', nareru gets used to, grows

197

familiar with

nari form ; personal appearance

narimas', naru[1] becomes, gets to be, turns into ; is completed ; is, amounts to

narimas', naru[2] (fruit) is borne

narimas', naru[3] it sounds, rings

naru-hodo I see ; quite so ; you are so right

nasake affection, feeling, tenderness, compassion

nashi pear

...-nashi without

nashimas', nasu achieves, forms, does

nasu eggplant

nata hatchet

natsu summer

natsu-mikan Japanese grapefruit

nawa rope, cord

naya barn, shed

nayami suffering, distress, torment

naze why

nazo riddle

ne 1. root 2. sound 3. sleeping 4. price

...ne! (nē!) isn't it, don't-you-know, you see

nebari stickiness

negaimas', negau asks for, requests, begs

neji screw

neji-mawashi screwdriver

neko cat

nekutai necktie

nemas', neru goes to bed, lies down, sleeps

nemmatsu the end of the year
nemui sleepy
nemurimas', nemuru sleeps
nen[1] year
nen[2] deliberation, attention
nenryō fuel
neraimas', nerau aims at, watches for, seeks
neru[1] **(nemas')** goes to bed, lies down, sleeps
neru[2] **(nerimas')** kneads
neru flannel
nē-san big sister ; Miss ; Waitress !
netsu fever ; heat
neuchi value, worth
nezumi mouse, rat
ni[1] two
ni[2] load, burden
...ni in, at ; to ; for ; with ; and
niaimas', niau is becoming, suits
nibui dull
Nichi- Japanese
nichiyōbi Sunday
ni-do two times
niemas', nieru it boils, it cooks   ⌈away
nigashimas', nigasu turns loose ; lets get
nigemas', nigeru runs away, escapes
nigirimas', nigiru grasps, grips, clutches
nigiyaka merry, bustling, lively, flourishing
Nihon Japan
Nihon-jin a Japanese

Nihongo Japanese (language)

Nihon-sei made in Japan

nii-san big brother

niji rainbow

ni-jū 1. twenty 2. double, duplicate

nikai 1. second floor, upstairs 2. two times

nikibi pimple

nikoniko smiling

niku meat

nikui dislikable, hated; hard, difficult

nikutai flesh, the body

nikuya butcher

nimas'[1], **niru** resembles

nimas'[2], **niru** boils, cooks

nimotsu baggage, load

nimpu coolie, workman

-nin person

ninaimas', ninau carries on shoulders

ningen human being

ningyō doll   ⌈heartedness

ninjō human nature, human feelings, warm-

ninki popularity

ninsoku coolie, workman

ninshin pregnancy

ninshin-chūzetsu abortion

nioi a smell

nira a leek; a green onion

niramimas', niramu glares, stares

niru[1] (**nimas'**) boils, cooks

niru² (nimas') resembles

nise phony, imitation

nishiki brocade

nishin herring

nisu varnish

ni-tō 2nd class

niwa garden

niwatori chicken

no (no-hara) field

... no 1. SUBORDINATING PARTICLE: of, pertaining to, in, at 2. = da which is 3. the one 4. (= koto) the fact, the act

nobashimas', nobasu; nobemas', noberu¹ extends it, reaches; spreads it

nobemas', noberu² tells, relates ⌈spreads

nobimas', nobiru it extends, reaches; it

noborimas', noboru climbs, goes up

nodo throat

nodo ga kawakimash'ta is thirsty

nōgyō agriculture

no-hara field

nokemas', nokeru removes; omits

noki eaves

nokogiri a saw ⌈(over)

nokorimas', nokoru remains, is left behind

nokoshimas', nokosu leaves behind (over)

nokimas', noku gets out of the way

nomi¹ chisel

nomi² flea

201

nomimizu drinking water
nomimono beverage, something to drink
nōmin the farmers
nomimas', nomu drinks
nonki easygoing, happy-go-lucky
noren shop curtain ; credit
nori 1. paste ; starch 2. seaweed
norikaemas', norikaeru changes (trains, buses, etc.)
norimas', noru gets aboard, rides
nōritsu efficiency
noroi slow, dull ⌈in
noru (norimas') gets aboard, rides ; is found
nosemas', noseru loads, puts aboard, ships ;
nōzei payment of taxes ⌊publishes
... nozoite except for, with the exception of
nozokimas', nozoku 1. peeps at 2. removes, eliminates ; omits
nozomashii desirable, welcome
nozomimas', nozomu desires, looks to, hopes for; looks out on ⌈etc.)
nugimas', nugu takes off (clothes, shoes,
nuguimas', nuguu wipes away
nuimas', nuu sews ⌈omitted
nukemas', nukeru comes off ; escapes ; is
nukimas', nuku uncorks ; removes ; omits ;
numa swamp, marsh ⌊surpasses ; selects
nurashimas', nurasu wets, dampens
nuremas', nureru gets wet, damp

202

nuri lacquer, varnish, painting

nurimono lacquerware

nurimas', nuru lacquers, paints, varnishes

nurui lukewarm ; sluggish

nushi master, owner

nusumimas', nusumu steals, swipes, robs

nuu (nuimas') sews

nyūbai the rainy season ⌈school

nyūgaku admission to a school, entering a

nyūin entering a hospital, hospital admission

nyūjō-ken admission ticket

nyūsu news

nyūyō necessary, needed

nyūyoku bath, taking a bath

O

o¹ (=shippo) tail

o² thong, strap (=hanao)

... O DIRECT OBJECT PARTICLE

o- HONORIFIC PREFIX: "your" or "that common thing we often talk about"

ō- big, great

oba(san) aunt ; lady

obā(san) grandmother ; old lady

obi belt, sash

oboemas', oboeru remembers

obuimas'. obuu carries on one's back

o-cha Japanese green tea

203

ochimas', ochiru falls; drops; is omitted; fails; runs away; is inferior ⌜cool
ochitsukimas', ochitsuku calms down, keeps
ōdan[1] jaundice
ōdan[2] crossing, going across, intersecting
odorimas', odoru dances
odorokimas', odoroku is surprised, aston-
oemas', oeru finishes, completes ⌞ished
ōfuku round trip ⌜respect
ogamimas', ogamu worships; looks at with
ōgata large-size (model)
ōgesa exaggerated
ogi a reed
ōgi a folding fan
oginaimas', oginau completes; comple-
ments; makes good, makes up for
ōgoe de in a loud voice ⌜person to
ogorimas', ogoru is extravagant; treats a
o-hachi a rice bucket
ohako hobby; specialty, trick
Ohayō (gozaimas')! Good morning!
o-hiya cold water
oi nephew
oi! hey!
ōi, ōku many, numerous ⌜stays
oide (ni narimas') 1. comes 2. goes 3. is,
oimas', ou[1] chases, pursues
oimas', ou[2] carries on back
ōimas', ōu covers, shields

204

oiru (lubricating) oil (*for car*)

oishii tasty, nice, delicious

oji (san) uncle

o-jigi a polite bow

ojii-san grandfather

ojoku disgrace, shame, scandal

ojō-san a young lady; your daughter

oka hill; dry land

okabu = ohako

okage sama de thanks to your kind attitude; thank you (I'm very well *or* it's going very nicely).

okame moonfaced woman

okami landlady, woman

ōkami wolf

o-kane money

okāsan mother

okashii amusing, funny

okashimas', okasu commits, perpetrates; violates, encroaches upon

ōkata 1. for the most part 2. probably

o-kawari 1. a second helping 2. change (in health)

okazu side dishes (*anything but rice*)

oke tub, wooden bucket

oki offshore

....-oki ni at intervals of ...

okiba a place (to put something)

ōkii, ōki na big, large

okimas',[1] oku puts ; does for later

okimas',[2] okiru gets up

okimono an ornament ; bric-a-brac

o-kome rice

okonaimas', okonau acts, does, carries out, performs ⌈from

okorimas', okoru[1] 1. happens 2. springs

okorimas', okoru[2] gets mad (angry)

okoshimas', okosu raises ; establishes ; gets a person up

okotarimas', okotaru neglects; is lazy about

ok'-san wife

oku[1] a hundred million

oku[2] the back or inside part

oku[3] (okimas') puts ; does for later

ōku lots ; mostly

okubi belch ⌈runs slow

okuremas', okureru is late ; falls behind ;

okurimono gift, present

okurimas', okuru 1. presents, awards with 2. sends ; sees a person off ; spends (time)

omake extra, bonus, premium; to boot

omaru bed-pan ; chamberpot

omawari-san policeman ⌈on back

ombu (shimas') carries baby on back ; rides

omedetō (gozaimas') congratulations; happy new year ⌈3. invites

omeshi (ni narimas') 1. wears 2. buys

omocha toy

206

omoi heavy; important
omoi-dashimas', -dasu remembers, recollects
omoimas', omou thinks, feels
omo na principal, main
omoshiroi interesting, pleasant, amusing, fun
omou thinks, feels
ōmu a parrot
omuretsu omelet
omutsu diapers
on[1] obligation; kindness
on[2] sound; pronunciation
onaji same
onaka stomach
onaka ga s'kimash'ta is hungry
onara flatulence, wind
ondo temperature
ongaku music
oni devil, ogre
onna woman, female
ono ax, hatchet
onore self
onozukara automatically, spontaneously
onsen hot spring
ōrai[1] traffic; communication; thoroughfare
ōrai[2] "all right" (all clear, go ahead)
Oranda Holland, Dutch
orenji orange, orange drink
oremas'. oreru it breaks; it folds
ori[1] time, occasion

207

ori[2] cage; jail

orime fold, crease, pleat

orimono textiles, cloth

orimas', oriru gets down, gets off

orimas', oru[1] is, stays=(**imas', iru**)

orimas', oru[2] breaks (folds, bends) it

orimas', oru[3] weaves

oroshimas', orosu takes down; unloads; invests; drops (from a car), lets out (of vehicle) ⌈trols

osaemas', osaeru represses, restrains, con-

o-sake=sake[1]

osamemas', osameru 1. reaps, harvests; gets 2. pays; finishes 3. governs; pacifies

oseji compliment, flattery

oshaberi chatterbox, gossip

oshare dandy, fancy dresser

oshiemas', oshieru teaches, shows, tells,

oshii 1. regrettable 2. precious ⌊informs

oshiire closet, cupboard

oshimas', osu pushes

oshiroi face powder

Ōshū, Europe

osoi late; slow

osoreirimas' 1. excuse me 2. thank you

osoremas', osoreru fears

osoroshii fearful, dreadful

osshaimas', ossharu (someone honored) says; is called

osu (oshimas') pushes
Ōs'torariya Australia
oto sound, noise
otoko man, male, boy
otona adult
otonashii gentle, well-behaved
otori decoy; lure   ⌜weak
otoroemas', otoroeru declines, fades, grows
otorimas', otoru is inferior, worse
otoshimas', otosu drops
otōto younger brother
ototoi day before yesterday
ototoshi year before last
otsu chic, stylish
ou (oimas')[1] chases, pursues
ou (oimas')[2] carries on back
ōu (ōimas') covers, shields
owarimas', owaru it ends
oya parent
oya-bun boss, ringleader, chief
ōyake public, open, official
oyatsu snack (esp. mid-afternoon)
ōyō application, putting to use
oyobi and also
oyobimas', oyobu reaches, extends to, equals
oyogimas', oyogu swims
ō-yorokobi de with great delight
oyoso about, roughly
ōzei large crowd, throng

P

pa...! all gone ; boom !
pachinko pinball
pāma permanent wave
pan bread
panku puncture, blowout
pan-s'ke pompom girl
pan-ya bakeshop
paripari crisp ; first-rate
pēji page
penki paint
pikapika flashing, glittering
pinto focus
poketto pocket
pomādo pomade, hair oil
pombiki a pimp, a hustler
posuto, pos'to a mailbox
potsu a dot
puro-resu professional wrestling ⌈ing lot
pūru 1. swimming pool 2. motor pool, park-

R

-ra and others ; all of
raigetsu next month
raikyaku guest, caller, visitor
rainen next year

raishū next week
rajio radio
raku ease, comfort, comfortable
rakudai failure (in a test)
rakugaki scribbling; doodling
rambō violence, outrage; disorderly
rāmen Chinese noodles
ramma transom window (opening)
ramune lemonade
ran 1. orchid 2. column
ranchi 1. lunch 2. launch
randoseru knapsack
rappa trumpet
...rashii probably; it seems like; it looks like
rebā 1. liver 2. lever
rei¹ (o-rei) greeting; thanks
rei² (maru) zero
rei³ precedent, example
reibō (-sōchi) air conditioning
reigai exception (to the rule)
reigi courtesy
reizōko refrigerator, icebox
rekishi history
rekōdo record
remon lemon
ren-ai love
renchū gang, crowd, clique
renga brick
rengō union, alliance, Allied

renraku connection ; relevancy

renshū training, practice. drill

ressha a train

retsu row, line

rettō archipelago, chain of islands

ri advantage, profit, interest

rieki benefit, advantage, profit

rihatsu-ten barbershop

rikai understanding, comprehension

rikō clever, sharp

riku land

rikugun army

rikutsu reason, logic, argument

rin a bell, a doorbell

ringo apple

rinji extraordinary, special, emergency

rinki emergency ; expedient

rippa fine, splendid ; well

rireki personal history, summary of one's ⌈career

rishi interest

risō ideal

risu squirrel

ritsu 1. rate, proportion 2. a cut, a per-

rittai solid; 3-D, stereoscopic ⌊centage

riyō use, utilization

riyū reason

rōdō-sha worker, laborer

roji alley

rōka passage, corridor, aisle

roku six

Rōma Rome

rōma-ji romanization, Latin letters

ron argument, discussion; treatise

rōnin an unemployed samurai; a boy between schools; a man without a job

ronri logic

Roshiya Russia

rōsoku candle

rōsu-biifu roastbeef

rōzu waste, refuse; damaged goods

rumpen tramp, hobo

rusu 1. absent, away from home 2. taking care of the house while one is away

rusu-ban someone to take care of the house in one's absence ⌈ens; omits

ryakushimas', ryakusu abbreviates, short-

ryō 1. hunting; fishing (as sport) 2. dormitory, boardinghouse 3. mound, mausoleum 4. territory 5. quantity

ryōgae money exchange

ryōhō both

ryōji (-kan) consul(ate)

ryokan inn

ryoken passport

ryokō travel, trip

ryokyaku traveler, passenger

ryōri cooking

ryōri-ten, -ya a restaurant

213

ryōshin[1] both parents
ryōshin[2] conscience
ryūkō popularity, vogue
Ryūkyū the Ryukyus (Okinawa, etc.)

S

sā well; come on
...sa! EMPHATIC PARTICLE
sabi rust
sabishii lonely
sābisu service; free (as part of the service)
saborimas', saboru cuts class; plays hookey
sadamarimas', sadamaru is settled, fixed
sadamemas', sadameru settles it, fixes it
...sae even; only   ⌈down
sagarimas', sagaru it hangs down; goes
sagashimas', sagasu looks for
sagemas', sageru 1. lets it hang down;
  lowers 2. carries (hanging)
sagurimas', saguru gropes
sai[1] talent, ability
sai[2] side-dish
sai[3] time, occasion
sai[4] wife
saiban trial, court decision
saichū midst
saifu purse
saigo last, final

saijō best, highest

saiku work(manship), ware

saishin newest, up-to-date

saisho the very beginning (first)

saishū final, the very end (last)

saiwai good fortune

saji spoon

saka hill, slope

sakan flourishing, prosperous; splendid, ⌈vigorous

sakana 1. fish 2. appetizers with liquor

sakasama upside down

sakazuki wine cup, saké cup

sake¹ saké (Japanese rice-wine)

sake² salmon

sakebimas', **sakebu** cries out, shouts

sakemas', **sakeru** avoids

saki 1. front; future; ahead 2. point, tip

saki-hodo a little while ago

sakimas', **saku** blooms, blossoms

sakku condom

sakura cherry tree

sakurambo a cherry

sam- **=san-**

... **sama** = ... **san** Mr., Mrs., Miss ⌈ers

samatagemas', **samatageru** obstructs, hind-

samayoimas', **samayou** wanders about

sama-zama diverse, all kinds

samemas', **sameru¹** wakes up, comes to
   one's senses

samemas', sameru² gets cold, cools off

sampo a walk

samui cold, chilly

san three

-san 1. Mr., Mrs., Miss 2. mountain

sangyō industry

sanka participation

sankaku triangle

sansei approval, support

santō third class

sao pole, rod

sappari 1. not at all 2. clean; fresh 3. frank

sara plate, dish; saucer; ashtray

sarada salad

saru monkey ⌈(do)

sasemas'. saseru makes (do), lets (do), has

sashi-agemas', -ageru presents; holds up

sashimas', sasu 1. points to; holds um
brella 2. stabs, stings

sasoimas'. sasou invites; tempts

satō sugar

satsu¹ a volume, a book

satsu² paper money, a bill

satsujin murder

sawagimas', sawagu makes lots of noise,

sawarimas', sawaru touches ⌊clamors

sayonara goodby

sebiro business suit

sei¹ height, stature

sei^2 1. nature 2. sex

sei^3 cause; due to...

-sei made in ...

seibu the west, the western part

seifu government

seifuku uniform

seiji politics

seikatsu life

seikō success

seinen young man, youth

seiryoku power, energy; influence

seisan production, manufacture

seiseki results, marks

seishiki formal, formality

seishin soul, mind, spirit

seishitsu character, disposition

seito pupil, student

seitō political party 　　　　 ⌈America

seiyō the West, the Occident, Europe and

seizei at most, at best

seizō production, manufacture

seizon existence

sekai world

seken the public, people, the world

seki^1 cough

seki^2 seat

Sekijūji Red Cross

sekinin responsibility, obligation

sekitan coal

217

sekiyu kerosene, petroleum
sekkaku especially ; with much trouble
sekken soap
semai narrow
sembei rice-crackers
semete at least ; at most
semmenki wash basin
semmon specialty, major (line)
sempō the other side
sempūki electric fan
sen¹ thousand
sen² line, route
sen³ plug, cork, stopper
sen⁴ (-to) cents
senden propaganda, publicity
sengetsu last month
sengo postwar
sen-in member of the crew ; ship's crew
senji wartime
senkyo election
senryō military occupation
sensei teacher ; Dr. ...
senshu athlete ; champion
senshū last week
sensō war, battle
sentaku¹ washing, laundry
sentaku² selection, choice
senzen prewar
seppuku harakiri

seri auction

serifu one's lines (in a play), dialogue

sētā sweater

setomono pottery, chinaware

Seto-naikai The Inland Sea

setsubi equipment, facilities

setsumei explanation

setsuna moment, instant

sewa 1. care, trouble, assistance 2. meddling, minding other people's business

-sha company

shaberimas', shaberu chatters

shabon soap

shaburimas', shaburu sucks, chews

shachō president of a company, boss

shadan corporation

shadō road, roadway, driveway

shagamimas', shagamu squats, crouches

sha-in employee   ⌊on heels

shakai society, social

shakkuri hiccup

shako garage, car-barn

shan pretty, handsome

share joke, pun

shashin photo, picture

shashō conductor

shatsu undershirt

shawā shower

shi¹ death

shi² = yon four

shi³ city

shi⁴ poetry

... shi Mr. ...

... shi, and

shiagemas', shiageru finishes up

shiai match, contest, meet

shiasatte three days from now

shiawase luck, fortune

shiba 1. turf, lawn 2. brushwood

shibai play (drama)

shibaraku for a while ⌈again.

Shibaraku des' ne. It's nice to see you

shibarimas', shibaru ties up

shibashiba often, repeatedly

shibiremas', shibireru goes numb, (a leg, etc.) falls asleep

shibori, o-shibori a wet towel (wrung out)

shiborimas', shiboru wrings out, squeezes

shibui 1. puckery, astringent 2. wry; glum 3. severely simple, tastefully bare

shichi¹ seven

shichi² something pawned

shichi-jū seventy

shichimen-chō turkey

shichiya pawnbroker, pawnshop

shichō mayor

shichū stew

shidai circumstances : as soon as
shidan army division
shidashiya caterer
shigai outskirts of city, suburbs
shigaretto cigarette
shigatsu April
shigeki stimulation
shigoto job, work, undertaking
shigure drizzle
shihai management, control
shiharai paying out
shihon capital, funds
shiji support, maintenance
shijin poet
shi-jū forty
shijū all the time
shika deer
...**shika** except for, only, but
shikaku. sh'kaku 1. square 2. qualification, competency
shikarimas', shikaru scolds
shikashi. sh'kashi but, however
shikata (sh'kata) ga arimasen there's nothing we can do about it
shiken, sh'ken examination, test
shikimono spread ; a rug, a cushion
shikkari firmly, resolutely
shikki dampness
shikko urinate (child's word)

221

shikimas', shiku spreads; sits on
shima[1] island
shima[2] stripes
shimaimas', shimau puts away, finishes
shimas', suru does
shimasen doesn't
shimash'ta did
Shimatta! Damn!
shimbun newspaper
shimemas', shimeru closes
shimerimas', shimeru is damp
shimeshimas', shimesu shows. indicates
shimi stain, blot
shimimas', shimiru penetrates, smarts
shimin citizen
shimo frost
shimpai worry, uneasiness
shimpo progress
shin 1. core, pith, heart 2. heart, spirit
shina articles, goods; quality
Shina China
shindai bed, berth
shingō signal
shinimas', shinu dies
shinja a believer; a Christian
shinjimas', shinjiru believes in, trusts
shinju pearl
shinkei nerve
shinnen new year

222

shinobimas', shinobu bears, puts up with
shinrai trust, confidence
shinri 1. psychology 2. truth
shinrui relative
shinsatsu medical examination
shinsetsu kind, cordial
shinu (shinimas') dies
shin-yō trust, confidence ; credit
shinzō heart
shio 1. salt 2. tide
shippai failure, blunder, defeat
shippo tail⎾amines
shirabemas', shiraberu investigates, ex-
shirami louse
shirase report, notice
shireikan commandant, headquarters
shiri buttocks, bottom, seat
shirimas', shiru knows
shiro (o-shiro) castle
shiroi white
shirōto amateur
shiru[1] juice, gravy ; broth, soup
shiru[2] (shirimas') knows
shirushi indication, sign, symptom ; effect
shiryo consideration, thought(-fulness)
shishi lion
shisō thought, concept
shita, sh'ta[1] bottom, below, under
shita, sh'ta[2] tongue

shita, sh'ta[3] did, has done
shitagatte according to, in conformity with
shitaku, sh'taku preparation, arrangement
shitashii intimate, familiar
shitate-ya tailor
shite, sh'te doing; does and
shiten branch shop
shitsu quality, nature
shitsubō disappointment
shitsugyō unemployment
shitsumon question
shitsurei discourtesy, impoliteness
shitsuren disappointment in love
shitte imas' knows
shiwa wrinkle, crease, fold
shiwaza act, deed
shiyō 1. use, employment 2. method, means,
shizen nature, natural
shizuka quiet, still
shizumimas', shizumu sinks
shō nature, disposition, quality
shōbai trade, business
shōben urine, urinate
shōbō fire-fighting
shōbu match, game, contest ⌐dealing with
shobun, shochi management, disposition,
shōchi agreement
Shōchi shimash'ta. Yes, sir.
shōchō symbol

224

shōga ginger
shōgai impediment, obstacle, hindrance
shōgakkō primary (elementary) school
shōgakusei primary school children
shōgi chess
shōgyō commerce, trade
shōhi consumption, spending
shōhin goods, merchandise
shoimas', shou carries on back, shoulders
shōjiki honest
shoki secretary
shōki sober; in one's right mind
shōkin 1. hard cash 2. prize money; reward
   3. indemnity, reparation
shokki table service (ware)
shokki-dana pantry, dish-cupboard
shokkō factory-worker; workman
shōko proof, evidence
shōkō commissioned officer
shoku 1. office, occupation 2. food
shokubutsu (botanical) plant
shokudō dining room; restaurant
shokudō-sha dining car, diner
shokuen table salt
shokugyō occupation, profession
shokuhin groceries
shokuji meal
shokumotsu food
shokuryō-hin groceries

shokuyoku appetite
shomei signature
shōnen boy, lad, youngster
shōni infant, child
shōnin merchant, trader
shōrai future
shōrei encouragement, stimulation, promo⌐tion
shori managing, disposing of, transacting, ⌐dealing with
shōryaku abbreviation
shōsa major; lieutenant commander
shosai study, library (room)
shoseki books, publications
shōsetsu fiction, novel
shōshō = chotto
shōsoku news, word from
shotai housekeeping; a household
shōtai invitation
shotchū all the time
shoten bookshop
shōten focus
shotō islands
shotoku income, gain
shotoku-zei income tax
shōtotsu collision
shou (shoimas') carries on back, shoulders
shōyo bonus, prize, reward
shoyū possession, one's own
shōyu soy sauce
shozai whereabouts

shū(-kan) week

shuchō shimas' asserts, claims, maintains

shudan ways, means, measures, steps

shūdan group, collective body

shufu 1. housewife 2. capital city

shugeki attack, charge

shugi principle, doctrine, -ism

shūi circumference; surroundings

shujin boss, master; husband

shuju all kinds of

shujutsu operation, surgery

shūkan custom, practice, habit

shukudai homework

shukuga congratulation

shū-kuriimu a cream puff, an eclair

shūmai small Chinese meat-filled pastries

shūmatsu weekend

shumi taste, interest

shunkan a moment, an instant

shuppan publishing

shuppatsu departure

shūri repair

shurui kind, sort

shūsen(-go) (after) the end of the war

shūshin ethics, morals

shūshoku getting a job

shusse making a success out of life

shusseki attendance, presence

shutchō a business trip, an official tour

shūten terminus

shuyō leading, chief

shūzen repair

sō 1. that's right, yes 2. that way, like that

Sō des' ka. 1. Oh? How interesting! 2. Is that right?

soba¹ side, near

soba² (**o-soba**) buckwheat noodles

sōbetsu farewell; send-off

soboku simple, naive, unsophisticated

sōchi equipment, apparatus

sochira 1. there, that way 2. that one

sōdan consultation, conference, advice, talk

sodatemas', sodateru raises, rears, educates

sodachimas', sodatsu grows up, is raised ⌊(reared)

sode sleeve

soemas', soeru adds, throws in extra, at-

sofu grandfather ⌊taches

sofuto(-kuriimu) "soft ice cream"=frozen

sōgo mutual, reciprocal ⌊custard

sōi discrepancy, difference

soimas', sou runs along, follows

soitsu that one

sōji cleaning, sweeping

sōji-fu cleaning lady (man)

sōji-ki a sweeper

sōjū shimas' manipulates, handles, con-

sōkei the grand total ⌊trols, operates

sokki shorthand

223

sokkuri entirely, completely; just like

soko[1] there, that place

soko[2] bottom

sokudo, sokuryoku speed

sokutatsu special delivery

somatsu crude, coarse

somemas', someru dyes

son damage, loss, disadvantage

sonaemas', sonaeru prepares, fixes, installs, furnishes; possesses

songai damage, harm

sonkei respect, esteem

sonna such (a), that kind of

sonnara then, in that case

sono that

son-shimas', -suru 1. incurs loss 2. exists

sonzai existence

soppa buckteeth

sora sky

sora de by heart, from memory ⌈2. warps

sorashimas', sorasu 1. dodges, turns aside

sore that one, it

soremas', soreru deviates, strays, digresses

Soren Soviet Russia

sori 1. warp, curve, bend 2. sled

sōri-daijin prime minister, premier

sorimas', soru 1. shaves 2. bends, warps

sōritsu establishment

soroban abacus, counting beads

229

soroemas', soroeru puts in order; collects;
soroi a set of something ⌊completes a set
soroimas', sorou are arranged in order;
 gather together; make a set
sōron quarrel, dispute
sorosoro little by little
soru (sorimas') 1. shaves 2. bends, warps
soshiki system, structure
sōshiki funeral
soshō lawsuit
sōshoku ornament, decoration
sosogimas', sosogu pours (into)
sōsu sauce; gravy
sotchi = sochira
soto outside, outdoors   ⌈er
sōtō 1. rather, quite, fairly 2. suitable, prop
...(ni) sotte along the ...
sou (soimas') runs along, follows
sōzō imagination
su 1. nest 2. vinegar
sū number; numeral
suashi barefoot
subarashii wonderful
subekkoi slippery, slick, smooth
suberimas' suberu, slides, slips, skates
subete all
sue 1. end, close 2. future
sufu staple fiber
sūgaku mathematics

sugata form, figure, shape
sugi cryptomeria, Japanese cedar
...-sugi past (the hour)
sugimas', sugiru passes; exceeds; overdoes
sugoi 1. swell, wonderful, terrific 2. dread-
sugoku terribly ⌊ful, ghastly, weird
sugu ni at once, immediately ⌈ses
suguremas', sugureru is excellent; surpas-
suidō waterworks, water service
suiei swimming
suifu seaman, sailor
suigara cigarette (cigar) butt
suihei¹ navy man, sailor, seaman
suihei² horizon; water level ⌈in
suimas', suu sips, sucks, smokes, breathes
suimin(-zai) sleep(ing pills)
suiyōbi Wednesday
suji tendon; muscle; fiber; line; plot
sūji numeral, figure
sukebe, s'kebe oversexed, wolfish
suki, s'ki¹ is liked
suki, s'ki²(-ma) crack; opening; opportunity
suki, s'ki³ a plow
sukimas', suku 1. likes 2. plows 3. combs
sukkari completely, all
sukoshi, s'koshi a little, a bit
sukunai few, meager
sukuimas', sukuu helps, rescues, saves
sumai residence

231

sumashimas', sumasu 1. finishes, concludes
2. puts up with (things as they are)

sumi[1] an inside corner

sumi[2] 1. charcoal 2. India ink

sumō Japanese wrestling

sumimas', sumu 1. comes to an end 2. lives

Sumimasen. 1. Excuse me. 2. Thank you.

sumpō measurements

suna sand ⌐in other words

sunawachi namely, to wit; that is to say;

sune shin, leg

supōtsu, s'pōts' sports, athletics

suppai sour

suremas', sureru it rubs, grazes

suri pickpocket

surimas', suru 1. rubs; files; grinds 2.
prints 3. picks one's pockets

suru (shimas') does

sushi (o-sushi) pickled-rice tidb

suso skirt (of mountain); hem

susu soot

susumemas', susumeru encourages, recom-
mends, advises, persuades, urges

susumimas', susumu goes forward, progres-
ses; goes too fast, gets ahead

sutando, s'tando a stand; gas station;
desk lamp, floor lamp

suteki, s'teki fine, splendid, swell

sutekki, s'tekki walking stick, cane

232

sutemas', suteru throws away, abandons
sutēshon, s'tēshon railroad station
suto, s'to (sutoraiki) strike
sutōbu, s'tōbu stove, heater ⌈in
suu (suimas') sips, sucks, smokes, breathes
suwarimas', suwaru sits (especially Japa-
suzu 1. tin 2. little bells ⌊nese style)
suzume sparrow
suzushii cool

T

ta rice-field
taba bundle, bunch
tabako cigarettes; tobacco
tabemas', taberu eats
tabemono food
tabi[1] Japanese split-toe socks
tabi[2] journey, trip
...tabi ni every time...
tabi-tabi often
tabun 1. probably, likely; perhaps 2. a lot
tachi nature, disposition
tachiba viewpoint, standpoint, situation
tachi-domarimas', -domaru stops, stands
Tachiiri Kinshi No Trespassing ⌊still
tachimas', tatsu 1 stands up; leaves 2.
⌊elapses 3. cuts off
tada 1. only, just 2. (for) free 3. ordinary

tadaima just now ; in a minute

Tadaima (kaerimashita)! I'm back! (said on returning to one's residence)

tadashii proper, correct, honest ⌈terruption

taema-naku, taezu continuously, without in-

taemas', taeru 1. bears, puts up with ; 2. ⌊ceases

taga a barrel hoop

tagai (ni) mutual(ly)

-tagarimas', -tagaru wants to, is eager to

tai- 1. versus, towards, against 2. big, great

tai[1] sea bream, red snapper

tai[2] form, style ; body

tai[3] belt ; zone

-tai wants to, is eager to

taifū typhoon

taigai 1. in general ; for the most part ; practically 2. probably, like, like as not

Taiheiyō Pacific Ocean

taihen 1. very, exceedingly, terribly 2. serious ; disastrous ; enormous

taii army captain ; navy lieutenant

taiiku physical education, athletics

taikai 1. ocean, high sea 2. mass meeting ;

taikaku body build, physique ⌊convention

taikei a system

taiken personal experience

taiko drum

taikutsu boring, dull

taiman negligent, careless, neglectful

234

taimen 1. sense of honor, "face" 2. inter-

taira even, smooth, flat ⌊view

tairiku continent

taisa 1. army colonel; navy captain 2. a

Taiseiyō Atlantic Ocean ⌊great difference

taisen a great war, a world war

taisetsu important; precious

taishi ambassador

taishi-kan embassy ⌈mense

tai-shita (-sh'ta) important; serious; im-

...ni tai-sh'te against; toward

taishō 1. general; admiral 2. contrast

taishū the general public, the masses; pop-

taisō calisthenics, physical exercises ⌊ular

Taiwan Formosa

taiya a tire

taiyō 1. ocean 2. sun 3. summary

taka 1. hawk 2. quantity

takai high; loud

takara a treasure

take bamboo

take-no-ko bamboo shoot

taki waterfall

taki-bi bonfire

taki-gi firewood, fuel

taki-tsuke kindling

takimas', taku makes a fire; cooks; burns

tako 1. octopus 2. kite 3. callus, corn

taku (takimas') makes a fire; cooks; burns

235

taku 1. house; husband 2. table, desk
takumi skill
tak'san, takusan lots
takuwaemas', takuwaeru saves up, hoards
tama 1. ball; globe; bulb; bullet 2. jewel;
  bead; drop 3. round thing; coin; slug
tama ni rarely, occasionally, seldom
tamago egg ⌈intolerable
tamaranai, tamarimasen can't stand it; is
tamarimas', tamaru it accumulates
tamashii soul, spirit
tamatama occasionally
tamatsuki billiards
tambo rice-field
tame 1. for the sake (good, benefit) of 2.
  for the purpose of 3. because (of)
tamemas', tameru accumulates it
tameshimas', tamesu tries, attempts, experi-
tammono draperies, dry goods ⌊ments with
tamoto sleeve; edge, end
tamochimas', tamotsu keeps, preserves
tampopo dandelion
tamushi ringworm; athlete's foot
tana shelf, rack
tane 1. seed 2. source, cause 3. material 4.
  secret, trick to it 5. subject, topic
tango words, vocabulary
tan-i unit
tani(-ma) valley

tanjōbi birthday

tanomimas', tanomu 1. begs, requests 2. relies upon; entrusts with 3. hires, engages (a professional man)

tanoshii pleasant, enjoyable

tanoshimimas', tanoshimu enjoys

tansan(-sui) soda water

tansu chest of drawers

tantei detective

tanuki 1. badger 2. sly person

tanzen=dotera padded bathrobe

taoremas', taoreru falls down, tumbles,

taoru towel   ⌊collapses

taoshimas', taosu knocks down, overthrows

tappuri fully, more than enough

tara cod (fish)

...-tara if

tarai tub, basin

tarappu gangway

tarashimas', tarasu 1. seduces; wheedles 2. hangs, dangles; drops, spills

taremas', tareru hangs down, dangles; drips

tarimas, tariru is enough, suffices

taru barrel, keg   ⌈laxed

tarumimas', tarumu gets slack (loose), re-

taryō large quantity

tashika, tash'ka for sure; safe

tashikamemas', tashikameru makes sure,

tassha healthy; skillful, good at ⌊ascertains

237

tasshimas', tassuru accomplishes; reaches;
tasū large number ; majority ⌐lieved
tasukarimas', tasukaru is saved ; is re-
tasukemas', tasukeru 1. helps 2. saves
tasuki a sleeve cord
tatakaimas', tatakau fights
tatakimas', tataku strikes, hits
tatami floor-matting
tatamimas', tatamu folds up
tate ni lengthwise, vertically
-tate (no) fresh from...
tate-fuda signboard
tate-mashi house extension, annex
tatemas'. tateru erects, builds ; sets up.
tatemono building ⌐establishes
tatoeba for example, for instance ⌐off
tatsu 1. stands up ; leaves 2. elapses 3. cuts
taue rice-planting
tawara straw bag ; bale
tawashi scrubbing-brush ; swab
tayori communication, correspondence, a
letter, word from
tayorimas', tayoru relies on, depends on
tazunemas', tazuneru 1. asks (a question)
2. visits 3. looks for
te hand, arm ; trick, move ; kind ⌐ing
...-te GERUND: does and, is and ; doing, be-
teate treatment ; reparation, provision : al-
tebukuro gloves ⌐lowance

238

tēburu table ; -kake table-cloth

tegakari a hold, a place to hold on ; a clue,

tegami letter ⌊the track of

tegata a note, a bill

te-gatai safe ; reliable ; steady

tegokoro discretion

teguchi way (of doing things), trick

tehazu arrangements

tehon model, pattern

tei- fixed, appointed

teian proposal, suggestion

teibō dike, embankment

teiden failure (stoppage) of electricity

teido degree, extent

teika the set price

teiki (no) fixed, regular, periodical

teikoku empire, imperial

teinei polite ; careful

te-ire repair ; upkeep

teisai appearance, get-up, form

teisha stopping (of a vehicle)

teishi suspension, interruption

teishoku the regular meal ; table d'hote

teishu host ; landlord ; husband

tejun order, procedure, program

tekazu trouble

teki enemy, opponent, rival

-teki a drop

tekido moderation

tekigi suitable, fit
tekisetsu appropriate, to the point
tekishimas', tekisuru is suitable, qualified
tekis'to, tekisuto text (book)
tekitō suitable
tekki(-ten) hardware (store)
tekkyō iron bridge
teko lever
te-kubi wrist
tema time; trouble
temae this side; me, I
temane gesture
temaneki beckoning
temawari personal effects; luggage
...-te mo even if...
tempi oven   ⌠shrimp
tempura anything fried in batter, especially
ten 1. point, dot 2. sky, heaven
-ten shop   ⌠person
tengu 1. a long-nosed goblin 2. conceited
te-nimotsu hand luggage
ten-in shop clerk
tenjō ceiling
tenki 1. weather 2. nice weather
tennen natural
Tennō (sama) the Emperor
tensai genius
tensei disposition, temperament
tenshi angel

te-nugui hand towel

te-ono hatchet

teppen top

teppō rifle

tēpu tape

tera Buddhist temple

terebi television

teremas', tereru feels embarrassed, awk-ward, flustered

terimas', teru it shines

tesage handbag

tesū trouble

tetsu iron, steel

tetsudaimas', tetsudau helps

tetsudō railroad

tetsugaku philosophy

tetsuzuki formalities, procedure

tettei-teki thorough

to door

tō 1. ten 2. rattan, cane 3. tower, pagoda

tō- 1. the current, the appropriate 2. east

Tō-a East Asia

tobashimas', tobasu lets fly; skips, omits; hurries

tobimas', tobu jumps; flies

tobira a door of a gate

toboshii scarce, meager, scanty

tobu (tobimas') jumps; flies

tōbun for the time being

tōchaku arrival

tochi ground; a piece of land

241

tochū on the way

tōdai 1. lighthouse 2. (T) Tokyo University

toden Tokyo streetcar service ⌐reports

todokemas', todokeru 1. delivers 2. notifies,

todokimas', todoku reaches; arrives

todomarimas', todomaru it stops; it remains

todomemas', todomeru stops it

todorokimas', todoroku roars, rumbles

toei metropolitan (run by the metropolis of

tōfu bean curd ⌊Tokyo)

togamemas', togameru blames, reproves, finds fault with

togarashimas', togarasu sharpens, points

togarimas', togaru gets sharp (pointed)

toge thorn

tōge mountain pass

togemas', togeru achieves, accomplishes

togimas', togu grinds, sharpens, polishes

tōhyō ballot, vote

tōi far-off, distant

toimas', tou inquires

toire(tto) toilet

tōka 10 days; 10th day

tokai city, town

tokashimas', tokasu melts (dissolves) it

tokei clock; watch

tōkei statistics ⌐undone; gets solved

tokemas', tokeru it melts (dissolves); comes

toki time

tōki 1. pottery, ceramics 2. registration

tokimas', toku 1. undoes, unties; solves 2. explains, persuades, preaches 3. combs

tokkuri saké bottle

tokkyū special express (train)

toko bed

tokonoma alcove in Japanese room ⌐time

tokoro 1. place 2. address 3. circumstance,

toku[1] 1. virtue 2. profit, advantage, gain

toku[2] (**tokimas'**) 1. undoes, unties; solves 2. explains, persuades, preaches 3. combs

toku[3] special

tokubetsu special, particular, extra

tokui 1. pride 2. specialty 3. customer

toku-nitō special 2nd class

tokushoku special feature, characteristic

tokushu (tokuyū) special, particular

tōkyoku the authorities ⌐overnight

tomarimas', tomaru 1. it stops 2. stays

tombo dragonfly ⌐person up overnight

tomemas', tomeru 1. stops it 2. puts a

tomimas', tomu is rich in

tomma idiot, fool

tomo together; company; friend

...to mo! Of course...

tomonaimas', tomonau accompanies

tōmorokoshi corn

tomoshimas', tomosu burns (a light)

tomu (tomimas') is rich in

243

tonaemas', tonaeru advocates; shouts; recites; calls; claims

tōnan southeast

tonari next-door, neighbor(ing)

tonde-mo-nai, (tonda) outrageous, terrible, shocking

ton-katsu breaded pork cutlet

to-ni-kaku nevertheless

toppatsu outbreak

tora tiger

toraemas', toraeru catches, seizes

torakku 1. truck 2. track

torampu playing cards

tori 1. chicken 2. bird

tori- VERB PREFIX: takes and...

... tōri just as ...

tōri avenue; passage; way (of doing something)

tori-atsukaimas', -atsukau handles, deals with

tori-awase assortment

tori-hiki transaction, deal, business

torii gate to a Shinto shrine

tori-keshimas', -kesu cancels, revokes

torimas', toru takes; takes away

tōrimas', tōru passes by, passes through; penetrates

toritsugi 1. answering the door 2. an usher 3. agency 4. transmit thing

tōrō a stone lantern

tōroku registration

tōron debate, discussion

toru (torimas') takes; takes swav

tōru (**tōrimas'**) passes by, passes through; penetrates

Toruko (**-buro**) Turkey; Turkish (bath)

toshi[1] 1. age 2. year

toshi[2] city

tōshimas', **tōsu** lets through (in), admits; shows in; pierces, penetrates

toshi-shita younger

. . . to sh'te (**shite**) as, by way of

toshi-ue older

toshiyori an old person

tosho-kan library (building)

tosho-shitsu library (room) ⌈(mulled wine)

toso spiced saké drunk at New Year's

tōsu (**tōshimas'**) lets through (in), admits; shows in; pierces, penetrates

to(t)temo terribly, extremely, completely

totonoemas', **totonoeru** regulates, adjusts; prepares

totonoimas', **totonou** is in order; is ready

totsuzen suddenly

totte handle

. . . ni totte for, to

totte kimas' (**kuru**) brings

totte ikimas' (**iku**) takes

tou (**toimas'**) inquires

tōwaku embarrassment, dilemma

Tōyō the East, the Orient

to yū which says; which is (called), called

tozan mountain climbing

tōzen naturally ; proper, deserved

tsū authority, expert

tsuba spit, saliva

tsubaki camellia

tsubame swallow (bird)

tsubasa wing

tsubo 1. jar 2. 6 sq. ft. ⌈is shut

tsubomarimas', tsubomaru is puckered up;

tsubomemas', tsubomeru puckers it up;

tsubomi flower bud ⌊shuts

tsubu grain ; drop

tsuburemas', tsubureru it collapses (smash-

tsubushimas', tsubusu smashes (crushes) it

tsuchi 1. earth, ground 2. hammer

tsūchi report, notice

tsue cane, walking stick

tsuge boxwood

tsugemas', tsugeru tells, informs

tsugi 1. next ; following 2. patch

tsugimas', tsugu 1. pours 2. patches 3. in-

herits, succeeds to 4. joins, grafts, glues

tsugi-me joint, seam

tsugi-tsugi one after another ⌈nity

tsugō circumstances, convenience, opportu-

tsui[1] 1. just now 2. unintentionally

tsui[2] a pair

tsuide 1. opportunity, convenience 2. order

tsuihō purge

246

tsui-ni at last ; after all

. . . ni tsuite about, concerning

tsūji 1. bowel activity 2. effect

tsūjimas', **tsūjiru** gets through ; communicates ; transmits ; connects, runs ; is understood ; is well versed in

. . . o tsūjite through the good offices of. . .

tsūjō usual, ordinary

tsuka 1. mound 2. hilt

tsukaemas'[1], **tsukaeru** serves ; is useful

tsukaemas',[2] **tsukaeru** is obstructed, clogged up, busy

tsukai, ts'kai 1. message, errand 2. messenger, errand boy ⌐handles

tsukaimas', **tsukau** uses ; spends ; employs,

tsukamimas', **tsukamu** seizes, grasps

tsukaremas', **tsukareru** gets tired

tsukemono pickles

tsukemas', **tsukeru** 1. attaches, sticks on, adds ; turns on (lights) ; puts on, wears ; applies 2. pickles ; soaks

tsuki, ts'ki moon ⌐ship

tsukiai association, social company, friend-

tsuki-aimas', **-au** associates with, enjoys the company of

tsuki-atarimas', **-ataru** runs into ; comes to the end of ⌐sticks it out

tsuki-dashimas', **-dasu** makes protrude,

tsuki-demas', **-deru** protrudes, sticks out

247

tsukimas',[1] **tsukiru** comes to an end, runs out

tsukimas',[2] **tsuku** comes in contact; sticks to; joins; follows; touches; arrives; burns, is on

tsukimas',[3] **tsuku** stabs, thrusts, pushes

tsukurimas', tsukuru makes; builds; writes

tsukuroimas', tsukurou repairs, mends

tsukushimas', tsukusn exhausts, runs out of; exerts oneself, strives

tsuma wife   ⌈marizes

tsumamimas', tsumamu pinches, picks; sum-

tsumamimono things to nibble on (with one's fingers) while drinking

tsumaranai worthless, no good

tsumari after all; in short

tsumarimas', tsumaru is clogged up, choked; is stuck; is shortened; is crammed

tsumbo deaf

tsume claw, nail, hoof

tsumemas', tsumeru stuffs, crams; cans

tsumetai cold (to the touch)

tsumi crime, sin, guilt, fault

tsumimas', tsumu 1. piles it up, accumulates it; deposits; loads 2. gathers, plucks,

tsumori expectation, intention   ⌊clips

tsuna rope, cord, cable

tsunagimas', tsunagu connects, links, ties

tsune usual, ordinary

248

tsuno horn (of an animal)

tsura face

tsurai painful, cruel

tsure company, companion ⌐panied by

tsuremas', tsureru brings along, is accom-

tsuri 1. (small) change 2. fishing

tsuriai balance, equilibrium, symmetry

tsurigane temple bell

tsurimas', tsuru[1] 1. hangs 2. fishes

tsūro passage, thoroughfare

tsuru[2] 1. vine 2. earpieces of glasses frame 3. string (of bow or violin) 4. handle

tsūshin correspondence; news

tsutaemas', tsutaeru passes it on to some-one else; reports, communicates; trans-mits; hands down

tsutawarimas', tsutawaru is passed on (reported, communicated, transmitted, handed down)

tsutomemas', tsutomeru 1. is employed, works 2. exerts oneself, strives

tsutsu cylinder, pipe; gun

tsutsumi 1. package, bundle 2. dike, em-bankment

tsutsumimas', tsutsumu wraps it up

tsutsushimi prudence, discretion

tsuttsukimas', tsuttsuku pecks at

tsuya gloss, shine

tsūyaku interpreter; interpreting

tsuyoi strong; brave

tsuyu 1. dew 2. rainy season 3. light soup

tsuzukemas', tsuzukeru continues it

tsuzukimas', tsuzuku it continues

tsuzumemas', tsuzumeru reduces, cuts down, summarizes

tsuzurimas', tsuzuru 1. spells 2. composes, writes 3. patches; binds; sews (together)

U

u cormorant (fishing bird)

ubaimas', ubau seizes, robs, plunders

uchi 1. house, home; family 2. inside; among

uchi- VERB PREFIX: hits and, takes and

uchiki shy, timid

uchimas', utsu strikes, hits; sends a tele-

uchiwa a flat fan ⌊gram; fires, shoots

ude arm

ude-kubi wrist

ude-wa bracelet

udon Japanese noodles

ue above, upper; on, on top of

ueki-ya gardener

uemas', ueru 1. plants, grows 2. starves

ugokashimas', ugokasu moves it

ugokimas', ugoku it moves

uguisu nightingale

uji family, clan; family name

ukabimas', ukabu floats

ukagaimas', ukagau 1. visits 2. asks a question 3. hears 4. looks for

ukai 1. cormorant fishing 2. detour

ukemas', ukeru receives; accepts; takes; gets; suffers

uke-tori receipt

uke-tsuke information desk; receptionist

ukimas', uku floats

ukkari absentmindedly

uma horse

umai 1. tasty, delicious 2. skillful, good 3. successful, profitable

umaremas', umareru is born

ume plum tree

ume-boshi pickled plum

umemas', umeru buries; fills up; plugs

umi 1. sea 2. pus

umimas', umu 1. gives birth to 2. festers

ummei destiny

umpan transportation

un fate, luck (on)

unagashimas', unagasu stimulates, urges

unagi eel

unazukimas', unazuku nods athletics

undō 1. movement 2. exercise; sports;

undō-ba, (-jō) gymnasium; athletic field

unga canal

unsō transportation

251

unten operation, running, working, driving
unten-shu driver, operator
uo fish
ura[1] back (side); lining; what's behind it; ⌈the alley
ura[2] bay
ura-girimas', -giru betrays
ura-guchi back door
urami grudge, resentment, ill will
uranai fortunetelling; fortuneteller
uremas', ureru it sells, is in demand; thrives; is popular
ureshii delightful, pleasant, wonderful
uri melon
uri-dashi (special) sale
uri-kake credit sales
uriko shopgirl; salesman; peddler; newsboy
urimas', uru sells
urimono something for sale
ūru wool
urusai annoying
urushi lacquer
usagi rabbit
ushi cow, cattle
ushiro behind; (in) back
uso lie, fib
usu mortar
usui thin, pale, weak
uta song; poem
utagaimas', utagau doubts

utaimas', utau sings ; recites

utsu (uchimas') strikes, hits ; sends a telegram ; fires, shoots

utsukushii beautiful

utsurimas'. utsuru 1. it moves, shifts, changes 2. is reflected, can be seen (through); is becoming

utsushimas', utsusu 1. moves (transfers) it; infects, gives another person a disease 2. copies; takes a picture of; projects a picture

utsuwa 1. receptacle 2. tool 3. ability

uttaemas', uttaeru accuses, sues

uttōshii gloomy, dismal

uwabaki slippers

uwabe surface ; outer appearances

uwa-gaki address

uwagi coat, jacket

uwagoto raving, delirium

uwaki fickle

uwasa rumor, gossip

uyamaimas', uyamau reveres, respects

W

wa circle ; wheel ; link ; ring ; loop

... wa as for (DE-EMPHASIZES PRECEDING [WORD)

wa- Japanese

wabi apology

wabishii miserable ; lonely
wadai topic of conversation
wa-fuku, wa-f'ku Japanese clothes
waga-mama selfish
wairo bribery ; graft
waisetsu obscenity
waishatsu shirt
wakai young
wakaremas', wakareru they part, separate ;
  it branches off, splits
wakarimas', wakaru it is clear (understood) ;
  understands ; has good sense
wakashimas', wakasu boils it   ⌈stance
wake 1. reason 2. meaning 3. case, circum-
wakemas', wakeru divides (splits, distributes) it ; separates them
waki side (of the chest)   ⌈springs forth
wakimas', waku[1] 1. it boils 2. it gushes
waku[2] 1. frame ; crate 2. reel
wakuchin vaccine
wampaku naughty
wan 1. bowl 2. bay
wana trap, lasso
wani crocodile, alligator
wanisu varnish
wan-wan bow-wow !
wappu allotment, instalment
wara rice straw
waraimas', warau laughs

ware oneself ; me

waremas', wareru it cracks, it splits

ware-ware we ; us ⌜relatively

wariai rate, percentage : comparatively,

waribiki discount

wari-kan going Dutch ; splitting the bill

wari-mae share, portion ⌜it

warimas', waru divides it, breaks it, dilutes

warui 1. bad 2. at fault

waru-kuchi(-guchi) abuse, scolding, slander

wasabi horseradish

washi 1. eagle 2. Japanese paper

wa-shoku Japanese food

wasuremono 1. leaving something behind
  2. a thing left behind

wasuremas', wasureru forgets ⌜testines

wata 1. cotton 2. (=**hara-wata**) guts, in-

wata-ire cotton-padded (garment)

watakushi, watashi I, me

watarimas', wataru crosses over

watashi-bune ferryboat

watashimas', watasu hands over, ferries

watashi-tachi we, us

Y

ya arrow

...ya and ; or

yā hi !, hello !

255

yabai dangerous (will get you into trouble)
yaban barbarian
yabo stupid ; rustic
yabu bush, thicket   ⌈frustrated
yaburemas', **yabureru** it tears, bursts; is
yaburimas', **yaburu** tears (bursts) it ; frustrates ; violates ; defeats
yachin house rent
yado (-ya) inn
yaei camp, bivouac

yagai out in the country, out doors, in the
yagate before long ; in time   ⌊field
yagi goat
yagu bedclothes ; over-quilt
yahari also ; either ; all the same
yaiba blade ; sword
yaji heckling
yakamashii noisy ; annoying ; over-strict
yakan teakettle
yake desperation
yakedo burn, scald (on the skin)
yakemas', **yakeru** it burns ; it is baked
yaki- roast   ⌈toasts) it ; is jealous
yakimas', **yaku** burns it ; bakes (roasts,
yaki-mochi 1. jealousy 2. toasted rice-cake
yakimono pottery
yaki-pan toast
yakkai trouble, bother
yakkyoku pharmacy

yaku[1] **(yakimas')** burns it; bakes (roasts, toasts) it; is jealous

yaku[2] approximately, about ⌈use, service

yaku[3] 1. office, post, duty 2. part, role 3.

yakuhin drugs; chemicals

yakume duty, function

yakunin government official

yakusho government office

yakuza no-good, worthless; coarse

yakuzai pharmaceuticals, medicines

yakyū baseball

yama 1. mountain 2. heap, pile 3. climax 4. speculation, venture

yamashii ashamed *or* guilty-feeling

yama-te, yamano-te uptown: the bluff area

Yamato Japan

yamemas', yameru stops it; abolishes; abstains from, gives up; resigns, quits

yami 1. darkness 2. disorder 3. black-marketing 4. anything illicit

yamimas', yamu it stops

yamome widow

yamu-o-enai unavoidable

yanagi willow

yane roof

yaoya greengrocer, vegetable market

yappashi also; either; all the same

... yara ... or something; what with ...

yari spear

yarimas', yaru 1. gives 2. sends 3. does

yarō scoundrel, so-and-so !

yasai vegetables

yasashii gentle ; easy

yasemas', yaseru gets thin

yashi coconut

yashin ambition; treachery ⌈nourishes

yashinaimas', yashinau brings up, rears ;

yasui 1. cheap 2. easy 3. likely to, apt to

yasumi rest, break ; vacation ; holiday

yasumimas', yasumu rests, takes time off ;
  stays away (from school) ; goes to bed,

yatoimas', yatou employs, hires ⌊sleeps

yatsu guy, fellow, wretch ; thing

yatto at last ; barely, with difficulty

yattsu eight

yawarakai soft, mild

yaya a little ; a little while

yayakoshii complicated ; puzzling ; tangled

yo 1. the world at large, the public 2. the
  age, the times ; one's lifetime 3. night

yo- four

yō¹ manner, way ; kind, sort

...no yō like, as if ; seems like

yō² (go-yō) 1. business 2. use, service 3.

yō³ gist ⌊going to bathroom

yō- Western ; American

yobi reserve ⌈2. invites

yobimas', yobu 1. calls , names ; summons

258

yobō precaution, prevention

yochi room, space, margin, leeway

yōdo iodine ⌜suit ; a dress

yōfuku, yōf'ku (Western-style) clothes ; a

yōfuku-ya tailor ; clothing shop

yogoremas', yogoreru gets soiled (dirty)

yogoshimas', yogosu soils, dirties, stains

yōgu tools, implements

yōhin imported goods

yohō forecast, prediction

yohodo considerably, a good deal

yoi[1] evening

yoi[2] = ii good

yōi preparation ; caution

yōiku bringing up, education

yoimas', you gets drunk ; gets seasick

yōji 1. business, errand 2. toothpick 3. in-

yōjin precaution, caution, care ⌞fant

yōka 8 days ; ·8th day

yoke protection, shelter, screen

yokei superfluous, unnecessary, uncalled for

yokemas', yokeru avoids, keeps away from

yōki cheerful, bright, lively

yokin deposit (of money), bank account

yokka 4 days ; 4th day

yoko width ; sidewise

yokochō sidestreet, alley ⌜intersects

yoko-girimas', -giru crosses, cuts across,

yoku[1] greed

259

yoku[2] 1. well 2. lots, much 3. lots, often
yoku- the next (day, etc.)
yokubarimas', yokubaru is greedy
yōkyū demand, claim, request
yo-mawari night watchman
yome bride
yomimas', yomu reads
yōmō wool
yon four
yondokoro-nai inevitable
yo-nin 4 people
yopparaimas', yopparau gets drunk
yoppodo considerably, a good deal
... yori that ; from ; since ⌜3. meet
yorimas', yoru 1. drops in 2. comes near
yorokobimas', yorokobu is happy, delighted
yoron public opinion
Yōroppa Europe
yoroshii very well ; excellent ⌜best wishes
yoroshiku, yorosh'ku one's regards, one's
Dōzo yoroshiku. How do you do.
yoru[1] night ⌜3. meet
yoru[2] **(yorimas')** 1. drops in 2. comes near
yosan budget, estimate
yōsan raising silkworms, silk farming
yosemas', yoseru 1. lets approach, brings
  near 2. collects, gathers 3. adds 4. sends
Yosh'! OK ! ⌞5. makes (a crease)
yoshi reason ; meaning ; circumstance ; means

yōshi forms, blanks, papers ⌈ing
yōshoku foreign (Western, American) cook-
yoshu foreign liquor
yoso somewhere else ; alien, strange
yosō expectation, presumption
yoshimas', yosu stops it
yōsu circumstances; aspect; appearance, look
yotamono hoodlum
yō-tashi business, errand
yotei expectation, plan
yōten gist, point
...ni yotte according to ; because of
yottsu four
you (yoimas') gets drunk ; gets seasick
yowai weak ; frail ; easily intoxicated
yoyaku reservation, subscription, booking
yōyaku gradually ; at last ; barely
yoyū room, leeway, margin, excess, surplus
yu (o-yu) hot water, bath ; hot tea
'yū (iimas') says ; *see also* **to yū**
yūbe last night
yubi finger ; toe
yūbi elegant, graceful
yūbin mail
yūbin-kyoku post office
yubinuki thimble
yubiwa ring
yubi-zan finger counting
yubune bathtub

261

yūdachi a sudden shower

yudan negligence, carelessness, remissness

yudanemas', yudaneru entrusts, commits

Yudaya-jin Jew

Yudaya-kyō Judaism

yue reason, grounds

yūkan evening paper

yuki snow

...-yuki bound for

yukkuri slowly; at ease

yūkō effective, valid

yuku＝iku goes

yume dream

yūmei famous

yumi bow (for archery)

yumi-gata curve, arch, bow

yūmoa humor, wit

yunyū import(ing)

yūran excursion

yūrei ghost

yuremas', yureru it shakes, sways, rocks, ⌜rolls

yūretsu 1. quality 2. boldness

yuri lily

yūri profitable, advantageous

yurimas', yuru shakes it

yurui loose, slack; lax, lenient; slow

yurushimas', yurusu allows, permits, lets; pardons, forgives

yūryoku strong, powerful, influential

yūshō victory, championship
yūshoku supper
yūshū melancholy
yushutsu export(ing)
yusō transport(ation)
yusuri blackmail, extortion
yutaka abundant, plentiful ; wealthy
yutte saying ; says and
yūutsu melancholy, gloom
yuwakashi teakettle
yūwaku temptation ; seduction
yuzu orange ⌈cedes ; is inferior
yuzurimas', yuzuru gives up ; gives in ;

Z

za 1. theater 2. seat
zabuton cushion to sit on
zadan chat
zai 1. lumber 2. material 3. talent 4. wealth
zai- (resident) in
zaibatsu the big financial groups
zaidan a foundation (philanthropical, etc.)
zaikai financial circles
zaimoku lumber, wood
zairu a mountain-climbing rope
zairyō raw material
zaisan property
zaisei finance

zakka miscellaneous goods, sundries
zambō slander
zange confession (of sins)
zankoku cruel, brutal
zannen regret, disappointed; too bad
zara-ni found everywhere, very common
zara-zara rough
zaseki seat
zashiki room, living room
zasshi magazine, periodical
zassō weeds
zatsu- miscellaneous; rough; coarse
zatto roughly; briefly
zehi 1. without fail, for sure 2. right or
zei tax, customs   ⌊wrong
zeikan customs, custom house
zeikin tax
zeitaku luxury, extravagance
zembu all
zemmai 1. spring, hairspring 2. fern
zemmen 1. the entire surface 2. the front
zemmetsu annihilation   ⌊side
zempō the front
zen- all, total, complete, the whole
zentai the whole body, the entirety
zento the future, prospects
zen-ya the night before   ⌈gether
zenzen completely, utterly, entirely, alto-
zeppeki precipice

264

zerii jelly
zetsubō despair
zettai absolute(ly)
zō[1] statue, image, portrait
zō[2] elephant
zōdai enlargement, increase
zōgan inlaid work ; damascene
zōge ivory
zōho supplement

zōka increase, growth
zoku[1] common, vulgar ; popular
zoku[2] rebel ; thief
zokugo slang
zoku-shimas', -suru belongs ⌈succession
zokuzoku one right after another, in rapid
zombun as much as one likes
zongai beyond expectations
zōni rice-cakes boiled with vegetables (eaten
  at New Year's)
zonjimas', zonjiru thinks, feels ; knows
zonzai slovenly, rough, careless, sloppy
zōri straw sandals
zorozoro in a queue, all lined up
zōsen ship building
zōshin promotion, betterment, increase
zōsho book collection, library
zotto with a shiver (of horror)
zu picture, drawing, map, diagram
zuan sketch, design

zubon trousers, pants

zubon-shita underpants, shorts

zuhyō chart, diagram

zuibun 1. fairly, rather 2. quite, extremely

zuihitsu essays

zuii voluntary, optional

zukai illustration, diagram

-zuki a lover of ..., a great ... fan

zukku canvas; duck

zukku-kutsu tennis shoes

zunō brains, head ⌐loose

zuremas', zureru slips out of place, gets

zurōsu panties; drawers

zuru cheating

zurui sly, cunning, tricky

... zutsu each, apiece

zutsū headache

zutto 1. directly 2. by far, much (more) 3. all through, all the time

zuzan sloppy, slipshod, careless

zūzūshii brazen, shameless, pushy

PART V
Writing Charts

NOTE: The following charts show the essentials of *kana* spelling. The squarish letters on the left are *katakana*, which is used to write foreign words and odd-sounding native words. The roundish letters on the right are the ones used for other words. In addition, modern Japanese use about 2000 characters of Chinese origin, called *kanji*. The first two charts show the simple syllables; the third shows those with the -y- element inserted. After these are notes on special combinations, such as long vowels and consonants. The Romanization in heavy black type is that used in this book. For some of the syllables, there are other ways of Romanizing them, and these are also shown, but in regular typeface.

ア あ a	カ か ka	サ さ sa	タ た ta	ナ な na	ハ は ha	マ ま ma	ヤ や ya	ラ ら ra	ワ わ wa	ン ん -n,-m.
イ い i	キ き ki	シ し shi sh' si	チ ち chi ch' ti	ニ に ni	ヒ ひ hi	ミ み mi	—	リ り ri	ヰ ゐ (wi)	
ウ う u	ク く ku k'	ス す su s'	ツ つ tsu ts' tu	ヌ ぬ nu	フ ふ fu f' hu	ム む mu	ユ ゆ yu	ル る ru	—	
エ え e	ケ け ke	セ せ se	テ て te	ネ ね ne	ヘ へ he	メ め me	—	レ れ re	ヱ ゑ (we)	
オ お o	コ こ ko	ソ そ so	ト と to	ノ の no	ホ ほ ho	モ も mo	ヨ よ yo	ロ ろ ro	ヲ を (wo)	

ガ ga	ギ gi	グ gu	ゲ ge	ゴ go
ザ za	ジ ji (zi)	ズ zu	ゼ ze	ゾ zo
ダ da	ヂ ji (di)	ヅ zu (du)	デ de	ド do
パ pa	ピ pi	プ pu	ペ pe	ポ po
バ ba	ビ bi	ブ bu	ベ be	ボ bo

キャ きゃ kya	キュ きゅ kyu	キョ きょ kyo	ギャ ぎゃ gya	ギュ ぎゅ gyu	ギョ ぎょ gyo
シャ しゃ sha / sya	シュ しゅ shu / syu	ショ しょ sho / syo	ジャ じゃ ja / zya	ジュ じゅ ju / zyu	ジョ じょ jo / zyo
チャ ちゃ cha / tya	チュ ちゅ chu / tyu	チョ ちょ cho / tyo	ヂャ ぢゃ ja / dya	ヂュ ぢゅ ju / dyu	ヂョ ぢょ jo / dyo
ニャ にゃ nya	ニュ にゅ nyu	ニョ にょ nyo			
ヒャ ひゃ hya	ヒュ ひゅ hyu	ヒョ ひょ hyo	ピャ ぴゃ pya	ピュ ぴゅ pyu	ピョ ぴょ pyo
			ビャ びゃ bya	ビュ びゅ byu	ビョ びょ byo
ミャ みゃ mya	ミュ みゅ myu	ミョ みょ myo			
リャ りゃ rya	リュ りゅ ryu	リョ りょ ryo			

Long vowels are usually shown by repeating the vowel when writing in hiragana:
ā ああ, kā かあ, ū うう, fū ふう, ii いい,
nii にい, ē ええ, tē てえ.

In katakana, a single long stroke is often used (especially for foreign words):
ā アー, kā カー, ū ウー, fū フー, ii イー,
nii ニー, ē エー, tē テー.

But in hiragana the long ō is usually written as if it were **ou** (for most, but not all, words):
ō おう, kō こう, sō そう, kyō きょう, yō
よう.

Long consonants (**pp, tt, tch, kk, ss, ssh**) are written by inserting **tsu**, usually written smaller than the other letters:
kippu きっぷ, **natte** なって, **botchan** ボッ
チャン, **gakkō** がっこう, **massugu** マッスグ,
issho いっしょ.

But long **-mm-** and **-nn-** are written with ん and the appropriate symbol from the **ma** or **na** columns:
ammari あんまり, **semmon** センモン, **annai**
あんない, **san-nen** さんねん, **sam-myaku** さ
んみゃく.